Mrs. Warren's Profession

By George Bernard Shaw

2

21.44

A Digireads.com Book
Digireads.com Publishing
16212 Riggs Rd
Stilwell, KS, 66085

Mrs. Warren's Profession
By George Bernard Shaw
ISBN: 1-4209-2893-7

Please visit *www.digireads.com*

THE AUTHOR'S APOLOGY

Mrs. Warren's Profession has been performed at last, after a delay of only eight years; and I have once more shared with Ibsen the triumphant amusement of startling all but the strongest-headed of the London theatre critics clean out of the practice of their profession. No author who has ever known the exultation of sending the Press into an hysterical tumult of protest, of moral panic, of involuntary and frantic confession of sin, of a horror of conscience in which the power of distinguishing between the work of art on the stage and the real life of the spectator is confused and overwhelmed, will ever care for the stereotyped compliments which every successful farce or melodrama elicits from the newspapers. Give me that critic who rushed from my play to declare furiously that Sir George Crofts ought to be kicked. What a triumph for the actor, thus to reduce a jaded London journalist to the condition of the simple sailor in the Wapping gallery, who shouts execrations at Iago and warnings to Othello not to believe him! But dearer still than such simplicity is that sense of the sudden earthquake shock to the foundations of morality which sends a pallid crowd of critics into the street shrieking that the pillars of society are cracking and the ruin of the State is at hand. Even the Ibsen champions of ten years ago remonstrate with me just as the veterans of those brave days remonstrated with them. Mr. Grein, the hardy iconoclast who first launched my plays on the stage alongside Ghosts and The Wild Duck, exclaimed that I have shattered his ideals. Actually his ideals! What would Dr Relling say? And Mr. William Archer himself disowns me because I "cannot touch pitch without wallowing in it". Truly my play must be more needed than I knew; and yet I thought I knew how little the others know.

Do not suppose, however, that the consternation of the Press reflects any consternation among the general public. Anybody can upset the theatre critics, in a turn of the wrist, by substituting for the romantic commonplaces of the stage the moral commonplaces of the pulpit, platform, or the library. Play Mrs. Warren's Profession to an audience of clerical members of the Christian Social Union and of women well experienced in Rescue, Temperance, and Girls' Club work, and no moral panic will arise; every man and woman present will know that as long as poverty makes virtue hideous and the spare pocket-money of rich bachelordom makes vice dazzling, their daily hand-to-hand fight against prostitution with prayer and persuasion, shelters and scanty alms, will be a losing one. There was a time when they were able to urge that though "the white-lead factory where Anne Jane was poisoned" may be a far more terrible place than Mrs. Warren's house, yet hell is still more dreadful. Nowadays they no longer believe in hell; and the girls among whom they are working know that they do not believe in it, and would laugh at them if they did. So well have the rescuers learnt that Mrs. Warren's defence of herself and indictment of society is the thing that most needs saying, that those who know me personally reproach me, not for writing this play, but for wasting my energies on "pleasant plays" for the amusement of frivolous people, when I can build up such excellent stage sermons on their own work. Mrs. Warren's Profession is the one play of mine which I could submit to a censorship without doubt of the result; only, it must not be the censorship of the minor theatre critic, nor of an innocent court official like the Lord Chamberlain's Examiner, much less of people who consciously profit by Mrs. Warren's profession, or who personally make use of it, or who hold the widely whispered view that it is an indispensable safety-valve for the protection of domestic virtue, or, above all, who are smitten with a sentimental affection for our fallen sister, and would "take her up tenderly, lift her with care, fashioned so slenderly, young, and SO fair." Nor am I prepared to accept the verdict of the medical gentlemen who would compulsorily sanitate and register Mrs. Warren, whilst leaving Mrs. Warren's patrons, especially her military patrons, free to destroy her health and anybody else's without fear of reprisals. But I should be quite content to have my play judged by, say, a joint committee of the Central Vigilance Society and the Salvation Army. And the sterner moralists the members of the committee were, the better.

Some of the journalists I have shocked reason so unripely that they will gather nothing from this but a confused notion that I am accusing the National Vigilance Association and the Salvation Army of complicity in my own scandalous immorality. It will seem to them that people who would stand this play would stand anything. They are quite mistaken. Such an audience as I have described would be revolted by many of our fashionable plays. They would leave the theatre convinced that the Plymouth Brother who still regards the playhouse as one of the gates of hell is perhaps the safest adviser on the subject of which he knows so little. If I do not draw the same conclusion, it is not because I am one of those who claim that art is exempt from moral obligations, and deny that the writing or performance of a play is a moral act, to be treated on exactly the same footing as theft or murder if it produces equally mischievous consequences. I am convinced that fine art is the subtlest, the most seductive, the most effective instrument of moral propaganda in the world, excepting only the example of personal conduct; and I waive even this exception in favor of the art of the stage, because it works by exhibiting examples of personal conduct made intelligible and moving to crowds of unobservant, unreflecting people to whom real life means nothing. I have pointed out again and again that the influence of the theatre in England is growing so great that whilst private conduct, religion, law, science, politics, and morals are becoming more and more theatrical, the theatre itself remains impervious to common sense, religion, science, politics, and morals. That is why I fight the theatre, not with pamphlets and sermons and treatises, but with plays; and so effective do I find the dramatic method that I have no doubt I shall at last persuade even London to take its conscience and its brains with it when it goes to the theatre, instead of leaving them at home with its prayer-book as it does at present. Consequently, I am the last man in the world to deny that if the net effect of performing Mrs. Warren's Profession were an increase in the number of persons entering that profession, its performance should be dealt with accordingly.

Now let us consider how such recruiting can be encouraged by the theatre. Nothing is easier. Let the King's Reader of Plays, backed by the Press, make an unwritten but perfectly well understood regulation that members of Mrs. Warren's profession shall be tolerated on the stage only when they are beautiful, exquisitely dressed, and sumptuously lodged and fed; also that they shall, at the end of the play, die of consumption to the sympathetic tears of the whole audience, or step into the next room to commit suicide, or at least be turned out by their protectors and passed on to be "redeemed" by old and faithful lovers who have adored them in spite of their levities. Naturally, the poorer girls in the gallery will believe in the beauty, in the exquisite dresses, and the luxurious living, and will see that there is no real necessity for the consumption, the suicide, or the ejectment: mere pious forms, all of them, to save the Censor's face. Even if these purely official catastrophes carried any conviction, the majority of English girls remain so poor, so dependent, so well aware that the drudgeries of such honest work as is within their reach are likely enough to lead them eventually to lung disease, premature death, and domestic desertion or brutality, that they would still see reason to prefer the primrose path to the strait path of virtue, since both, vice at worst and virtue at best, lead to the same end in poverty and overwork. It is true that the Board School mistress will tell you that only girls of a certain kind will reason in this way. But alas! that certain kind turns out on inquiry to be simply the pretty, dainty kind: that is, the only kind that gets the chance of acting on such reasoning. Read the first report of the Commission on the Housing of the Working Classes [Bluebook C 4402, 8d., 1889]; read the Report on Home Industries (sacred word, Home!) issued by the Women's Industrial Council [Home Industries of Women in London, 1897, 1s., 12 Buckingham Street, W. C.]; and ask yourself whether, if the lot in life therein described were your lot in life, you would not prefer the lot of Cleopatra, of Theodora, of the Lady of the Camellias, of Mrs. Tanqueray, of Zaza, of Iris. If you can go deep enough into things to be able to say no, how many ignorant half-starved girls will believe you are speaking sincerely? To them the lot of Iris is heavenly in comparison with their own. Yet our King, like his predecessors, says to the dramatist, "Thus, and thus only, shall you present Mrs. Warren's profession on the stage, or you shall starve. Witness Shaw, who told the untempting truth about it, and whom We, by the Grace of God, accordingly disallow and suppress, and do what in Us lies to silence." Fortunately, Shaw cannot be silenced. "The harlot's cry from street to street" is louder than the voices of all the kings. I am not dependent on the theatre, and cannot be starved into making my play a standing advertisement of the attractive side of Mrs. Warren's business.

Here I must guard myself against a misunderstanding. It is not the fault of their authors that the long string of wanton's tragedies, from Antony and Cleopatra to Iris, are snares to poor girls, and are objected to on that account by many earnest men and women who consider Mrs. Warren's Profession an excellent sermon. Mr. Pinero is in no way bound to suppress the fact that his Iris is a person to be envied by millions of better women. If he made his play false to life by inventing fictitious disadvantages for her, he would be acting as unscrupulously as any tract writer. If society chooses to provide for its Irises better than for its working women, it must not expect honest playwrights to manufacture spurious evidence to save its credit. The mischief lies in the deliberate suppression of the other side of the case: the refusal to allow Mrs. Warren to expose the drudgery and repulsiveness of plying for hire among coarse, tedious drunkards; the determination not to let the Parisian girl in Brieux's Les Avaries come on the stage and drive into people's minds what her diseases mean for her and for themselves. All that, says the King's Reader in effect, is horrifying, loathsome.

Precisely: what does he expect it to be? would he have us represent it as beautiful and gratifying? The answer to this question, I fear, must be a blunt Yes; for it seems impossible to root out of an Englishman's mind the notion that vice is delightful, and that abstention from it is privation. At all events, as long as the tempting side of it is kept towards the public, and softened by plenty of sentiment and sympathy, it is welcomed by our Censor, whereas the slightest attempt to place it in the light of the policeman's lantern or the Salvation Army shelter is checkmated at once as not merely disgusting, but, if you please, unnecessary.

Everybody will, I hope, admit that this state of things is intolerable; that the subject of Mrs. Warren's profession must be either tapu altogether, or else exhibited with the warning side as freely displayed as the tempting side. But many persons will vote for a complete tapu, and an impartial sweep from the boards of Mrs. Warren and Gretchen and the rest; in short, for banishing the sexual instincts from the stage altogether. Those who think this impossible can hardly have considered the number and importance of the subjects which are actually banished from the stage. Many plays, among them Lear, Hamlet, Macbeth, Coriolanus, Julius Caesar, have no sex complications: the thread of their action can be followed by children who could not understand a single scene of Mrs. Warren's Profession or Iris. None of our plays rouse the sympathy of the audience by an exhibition of the pains of maternity, as Chinese plays constantly do. Each nation has its own particular set of tapus in addition to the common human stock; and though each of these tapus limits the scope of the dramatist, it does not make drama impossible. If the Examiner were to refuse to license plays with female characters in them, he would only be doing to the stage what our tribal customs already do to the pulpit and the bar. I have myself written a rather entertaining play with only one woman in it, and she is quite heartwhole; and I could just as easily write a play without a woman in it at all. I will even go so far as to promise the Mr. Redford my support if he will introduce this limitation for part of the year, say during Lent, so as to make a close season for that dullest of stock dramatic subjects, adultery, and force our managers and authors to find out what all great dramatists find out spontaneously: to wit, that people who sacrifice every other consideration to love are as hopelessly unheroic on the stage as lunatics or dipsomaniacs. Hector is the world's hero; not Paris nor Antony.

But though I do not question the possibility of a drama in which love should be as effectively ignored as cholera is at present, there is not the slightest chance of that way out of the difficulty being taken by the Mr. Redford. If he attempted it there would be a revolt in which he would be swept away in spite of my singlehanded efforts to defend him. A complete tapu is politically impossible. A complete toleration is equally impossible to Mr. Redford, because his occupation would be gone if there were no tapu to enforce. He is therefore compelled to maintain the present compromise of a partial tapu, applied, to the best of his judgement, with a careful respect to persons and to public opinion. And a very sensible English solution of the difficulty, too, most readers will say. I should not dispute it if dramatic poets really were what English public opinion generally assumes them to be during their lifetime: that is, a licentiously irregular group to be kept in order in a rough and ready way by a magistrate who will stand no nonsense from them. But I cannot admit that the class represented by Eschylus, Sophocles, Aristophanes, Euripides, Shakespeare, Goethe, Ibsen, and Tolstoy, not to mention our own contemporary playwrights, is as much in place in Mr. Redford's office as a pickpocket is in Bow Street. Further, it is not true that the Censorship, though it certainly suppresses Ibsen and Tolstoy, and would suppress Shakespeare but for the absurd rule that a play once licensed is always licensed (so that Wycherly is permitted and Shelley prohibited), also suppresses unscrupulous playwrights. I challenge Mr. Redford to mention any extremity of sexual misconduct which any manager in his senses would risk presenting on the London stage that has not been presented under his license and that of his predecessor. The compromise, in fact, works out in practice in favor of loose plays as against earnest ones.

To carry conviction on this point, I will take the extreme course of narrating the plots of two plays witnessed within the last ten years by myself at London West End theatres, one licensed by the late Queen Victoria's Reader of Plays, the other by the present Reader to the King. Both plots conform to the strictest rules of the period when La Dame aux Camellias was still a forbidden play, and when The Second Mrs. Tanqueray would have been tolerated only on condition that she carefully explained to the audience that when she met Captain Ardale she sinned "but in intention."

Play number one. A prince is compelled by his parents to marry the daughter of a neighboring king, but loves another maiden. The scene represents a hall in the king's palace at night. The wedding has taken place that day; and the closed door of the nuptial chamber is in view of the audience. Inside, the princess awaits her bridegroom. A duenna is in attendance. The bridegroom enters. His sole desire is to escape from a marriage which is hateful to him. An idea strikes him. He will assault the duenna, and get ignominiously expelled from the palace by his indignant father-in-law. To his horror, when he proceeds to carry out this stratagem, the duenna, far from raising an alarm, is flattered, delighted, and compliant. The assaulter becomes the assaulted. He flings her angrily to the ground, where she remains placidly. He flies. The father enters; dismisses the duenna; and listens at the keyhole of his daughter's nuptial chamber, uttering various pleasantries, and declaring, with a shiver, that a sound of kissing, which he supposes to proceed from within, makes him feel young again.

In deprecation of the scandalized astonishment with which such a story as this will be read, I can only say that it was not presented on the stage until its propriety had been certified by the chief officer of the Queen of England's household.

Story number two. A German officer finds himself in an inn with a French lady who has wounded his national vanity. He resolves to humble her by committing a rape upon her. He announces his purpose. She remonstrates, implores, flies to the doors and finds them locked, calls for help and finds none at hand, runs screaming from side to side, and, after a harrowing scene, is overpowered and faints. Nothing further being possible on the stage without actual felony, the officer then relents and leaves her. When she recovers, she believes that he has carried out his threat; and during the rest of the play she is represented as vainly vowing vengeance upon him, whilst she is really falling in love with him under the influence of his imaginary crime against her. Finally she consents to marry him; and the curtain falls on their happiness.

This story was certified by the present King's Reader, acting for the Lord Chamberlain, as void in its general tendency of "anything immoral or otherwise improper for the stage." But let nobody conclude therefore that Mr. Redford is a monster, whose policy it is to deprave the theatre. As a matter of fact, both the above stories are strictly in order from the official point of view. The incidents of sex which they contain, though carried in both to the extreme point at which another step would be dealt with, not by the King's Reader, but by the police, do not involve adultery, nor any allusion to Mrs. Warren's profession, nor to the fact that the children of any polyandrous group will, when they grow up, inevitably be confronted, as those of Mrs. Warren's group are in my play, with the insoluble problem of their own possible consanguinity. In short, by depending wholly on the coarse humors and the physical fascination of sex, they comply with all the formulable requirements of the Censorship, whereas plays in which these humors and fascinations are discarded, and the social problems created by sex seriously faced and dealt with, inevitably ignore the official formula and are suppressed. If the old rule against the exhibition of illicit sex relations on stage were revived, and the subject absolutely barred, the only result would be that Antony and Cleopatra, Othello (because of the Bianca episode), Troilus and Cressida, Henry IV, Measure for Measure, Timon of Athens, La Dame aux Camellias, The Profligate,

The Second Mrs. Tanqueray, The Notorious Mrs. Ebbsmith, The Gay Lord Quex, Mrs. Dane's Defence, and Iris would be swept from the stage, and placed under the same ban as Tolstoy's Dominion of Darkness and Mrs. Warren's Profession, whilst such plays as the two described above would have a monopoly of the theatre as far as sexual interest is concerned.

What is more, the repulsiveness of the worst of the certified plays would protect the Censorship against effective exposure and criticism. Not long ago an American Review of high standing asked me for an article on the Censorship of the English stage. I replied that such an article would involve passages too disagreeable for publication in a magazine for general family reading. The editor persisted nevertheless; but not until he had declared his readiness to face this, and had pledged himself to insert the article unaltered (the particularity of the pledge extending even to a specification of the exact number of words in the article) did I consent to the proposal. What was the result?

The editor, confronted with the two stories given above, threw his pledge to the winds, and, instead of returning the article, printed it with the illustrative examples omitted, and nothing left but the argument from political principles against the Censorship. In doing this he fired my broadside after withdrawing the cannon balls; for neither the Censor nor any other Englishman, except perhaps Mr. Leslie Stephen and a few other veterans of the dwindling old guard of Benthamism, cares a dump about political principle. The ordinary Briton thinks that if every other Briton is not kept under some form of tutelage, the more childish the better, he will abuse his freedom viciously. As far as its principle is concerned, the Censorship is the most popular institution in England; and the playwright who criticizes it is slighted as a blackguard agitating for impunity. Consequently nothing can really shake the confidence of the public in the Lord Chamberlain's department except a remorseless and unbowdlerized narration of the licentious fictions which slip through its net, and are hallmarked by it with the approval of the Throne. But since these narrations cannot be made public without great difficulty, owing to the obligation an editor is under not to deal unexpectedly with matters that are not virginibus puerisque, the chances are heavily in favor of the Censor escaping all remonstrance. With the exception of such comments as I was able to make in my own critical articles in The World and The Saturday Review when the pieces I have described were first produced, and a few ignorant protests by churchmen against much better plays which they confessed they had not seen nor read, nothing has been said in the press that could seriously disturb the easygoing notion that the stage would be much worse than it admittedly is but for the vigilance of the King's Reader. The truth is, that no manager would dare produce on his own responsibility the pieces he can now get royal certificates for at two guineas per piece.

I hasten to add that I believe these evils to be inherent in the nature of all censorship, and not merely a consequence of the form the institution takes in London. No doubt there is a staggering absurdity in appointing an ordinary clerk to see that the leaders of European literature do not corrupt the morals of the nation, and to restrain Sir Henry Irving, as a rogue and a vagabond, from presuming to impersonate Samson or David on the stage, though any other sort of artist may daub these scriptural figures on a signboard or carve them on a tombstone without hindrance. If the General Medical Council, the Royal College of Physicians, the Royal Academy of Arts, the Incorporated Law Society, and Convocation were abolished, and their functions handed over to the Mr. Redford, the Concert of Europe would presumably declare England mad, and treat her accordingly. Yet, though neither medicine nor painting nor law nor the Church moulds the character of the nation as potently as the theatre does, nothing can come on the stage unless its dimensions admit of its passing through Mr. Redford's mind! Pray do not think that I question Mr. Redford's honesty. I am quite sure that he sincerely thinks me a blackguard, and my play a grossly improper one, because, like Tolstoy's Dominion of Darkness, it produces, as they are both meant to produce, a very strong and very painful impression of evil. I do not doubt for a moment that the rapine play which I have described, and which he licensed, was quite incapable in manuscript of producing any particular effect on his mind at all, and that when he was once satisfied that the ill-conducted hero was a German and not an English officer, he passed the play without studying its moral tendencies. Even if he had undertaken that study, there is no more reason to suppose that he is a competent moralist than there is to suppose that I am a competent mathematician. But truly it does not matter whether he is a moralist or not. Let nobody dream for a moment that what is wrong with the Censorship is the shortcoming of the gentleman who happens at any moment to be acting as Censor. Replace him to-morrow by an Academy of Letters and an Academy of Dramatic Poetry, and the new and enlarged filter will still exclude original and epoch-making work, whilst passing conventional, old-fashioned, and vulgar work without question. The conclave which compiles the index of the Roman Catholic Church is the most august, ancient, learned, famous, and authoritative censorship in Europe. Is it more enlightened, more liberal, more tolerant that the comparatively infinitesimal office of the Lord Chamberlain? On the contrary, it has reduced itself to a degree of absurdity which makes a Catholic university a contradiction in terms. All censorships exist to prevent anyone from challenging current conceptions and existing institutions. All progress is initiated by challenging current concepts, and executed by supplanting existing institutions. Consequently the first condition of progress is the removal of censorships. There is the whole case against censorships in a nutshell.

It will be asked whether theatrical managers are to be allowed to produce what they like, without regard to the public interest. But that is not the alternative. The managers of our London music-halls are not subject to any censorship. They produce their entertainments on their own responsibility, and have no two-guinea certificates to plead if their houses are conducted viciously. They know that if they lose their character, the County Council will simply refuse to renew their license at the end of the year; and nothing in the history of popular art is more amazing than the improvement in music-halls that this simple arrangement has produced within a few years. Place the theatres on the same footing, and we shall promptly have a similar revolution: a whole class of frankly blackguardly plays, in which unscrupulous low comedians attract crowds to gaze at bevies of girls who have nothing to exhibit but their prettiness, will vanish like the obscene songs which were supposed to enliven the squalid dulness, incredible to the younger generation, of the music-halls fifteen years ago. On the other hand, plays which treat sex questions as problems for thought instead of as aphrodisiacs will be freely performed. Gentlemen of Mr. Redford's way of thinking will have plenty of opportunity of protesting against them in Council; but the result will be that the Mr. Redford will find his natural level; Ibsen and Tolstoy theirs; so no harm will be done.

This question of the Censorship reminds me that I have to apologize to those who went to the recent performance of Mrs. Warren's Profession expecting to find it what I have just called an aphrodisiac. That was not my fault; it was Mr. Redford's. After the specimens I have given of the tolerance of his department, it was natural enough for thoughtless people to infer that a play which overstepped his indulgence must be a very exciting play indeed. Accordingly, I find one critic so explicit as to the nature of his disappointment as to say candidly that "such airy talk as there is upon the matter is utterly unworthy of acceptance as being a representation of what people with blood in them think or do on such occasions." Thus am I crushed between the upper millstone of the Mr. Redford, who thinks me a libertine, and the nether popular critic, who thinks me a prude. Critics of all grades and ages, middle-aged fathers of families no less than ardent young enthusiasts, are equally indignant with me. They revile me as lacking in passion, in feeling, in manhood. Some of them even sum the matter up by denying me any dramatic power: a melancholy betrayal of what dramatic power has come to mean on our stage under the Censorship! Can I be expected to refrain from laughing at the spectacle of a number of respectable gentlemen lamenting because a playwright lures them to the theatre by a promise to excite their senses in a very special and sensational manner, and then, having successfully trapped them in exceptional numbers, proceeds to ignore their senses and ruthlessly improve their minds? But I protest again that the lure was not mine. The play had been in print for four years; and I have spared no pains to make known that my plays are built to induce, not voluptuous reverie but intellectual interest, not romantic rhapsody but humane concern. Accordingly, I do not find those critics who are gifted with intellectual appetite and political conscience complaining of want of dramatic power. Rather do they protest, not altogether unjustly, against a few relapses into staginess and caricature which betray the young playwright and the old playgoer in this early work of mine.

As to the voluptuaries, I can assure them that the playwright, whether he be myself or another, will always disappoint them. The drama can do little to delight the senses: all the apparent instances to the contrary are instances of the personal fascination of the performers. The drama of pure feeling is no longer in the hands of the playwright: it has been conquered by the musician, after whose enchantments all the verbal arts seem cold and tame. Romeo and Juliet with the loveliest Juliet is dry, tedious, and rhetorical in comparison with Wagner's Tristan, even though Isolde be both fourteen stone and forty, as she often is in Germany. Indeed, it needed no Wagner to convince the public of this. The voluptuous sentimentality of Gounod's Faust and Bizet's Carmen has captured the common playgoer; and there is, flatly, no future now for any drama without music except the drama of thought. The attempt to produce a genus of opera without music (and this absurdity is what our fashionable theatres have been driving at for a long time without knowing it) is far less hopeful than my own determination to accept problem as the normal materiel of the drama.

That this determination will throw me into a long conflict with our theatre critics, and with the few playgoers who go to the theatre as often as the critics, I well know; but I am too well equipped for the strife to be deterred by it, or to bear malice towards the losing side. In trying to produce the sensuous effects of opera, the fashionable drama has become so flaccid in its sentimentality, and the intellect of its frequenters so atrophied by disuse, that the reintroduction of problem, with its remorseless logic and iron framework of fact, inevitably produces at first an overwhelming impression of coldness and inhuman rationalism. But this will soon pass away. When the intellectual muscle and moral nerve of the critics has been developed in the struggle with modern problem plays, the pettish luxuriousness of the clever ones, and the sulky sense of disadvantaged weakness in the sentimental ones, will clear away; and it will be seen that only in the problem play is there any real drama, because drama is no mere setting up of the camera to nature: it is the presentation in parable of the conflict between Man's will and his environment: in a word, of problem. The vapidness of such drama as the pseudo-operatic plays contain lies in the fact that in them animal passion, sentimentally diluted, is shewn in conflict, not with real circumstances, but with a set of conventions and assumptions half of which do not exist off the stage, whilst the other half can either be evaded by a pretence of compliance or defied with complete impunity by any reasonably strong-minded person. Nobody can feel that such conventions are really compulsory; and consequently nobody can believe in the stage pathos that accepts them as an inexorable fate, or in the genuineness of the people who indulge in such pathos. Sitting at such plays, we do not believe: we make-believe. And the habit of make-believe becomes at last so rooted that criticism of the theatre insensibly ceases to be criticism at all, and becomes more and more a chronicle of the fashionable enterprises of the only realities left on the stage: that is, the performers in their own persons. In this phase the playwright who attempts to revive genuine drama produces the disagreeable impression of the pedant who attempts to start a serious discussion at a fashionable at-home. Later on, when he has driven the tea services out and made the people who had come to use the theatre as a drawing-room understand that it is they and not the dramatist who are the intruders, he has to face the accusation that his plays ignore human feeling, an illusion produced by that very resistance of fact and law to human feeling which creates drama. It is the deus ex machina who, by suspending that resistance, makes the fall of the curtain an immediate necessity, since drama ends exactly where resistance ends. Yet the introduction of this resistance produces so strong an impression of heartlessness nowadays that a distinguished critic has summed up the impression made on him by Mrs. Warren's Profession, by declaring that "the difference between the spirit of Tolstoy and the spirit of Mr. Shaw is the difference between the spirit of Christ and the spirit of Euclid." But the epigram would be as good if Tolstoy's name were put in place of mine and D'Annunzio's in place of Tolstoy. At the same time I accept the enormous compliment to my reasoning powers with sincere complacency; and I promise my flatterer that when he is sufficiently accustomed to and therefore undazzled by problem on the stage to be able to attend to the familiar factor of humanity in it as well as to the unfamiliar one of a real environment, he will both see and feel that Mrs. Warren's Profession is no mere theorem, but a play of instincts and temperaments in conflict with each other and with a flinty social problem that never yields an inch to mere sentiment.

I go further than this. I declare that the real secret of the cynicism and inhumanity of which shallower critics accuse me is the unexpectedness with which my characters behave like human beings, instead of conforming to the romantic logic of the stage. The axioms and postulates of that dreary mimanthropometry are so well known that it is almost impossible for its slaves to write tolerable last acts to their plays, so conventionally do their conclusions follow from their premises. Because I have thrown this logic ruthlessly overboard, I am accused of ignoring, not stage logic, but, of all things, human feeling. People with completely theatrified imaginations tell me that no girl would treat her mother as Vivie Warren does, meaning that no stage heroine would in a popular sentimental play. They say this just as they might say that no two straight lines would enclose a space. They do not see how completely inverted their vision has become even when I throw its preposterousness in their faces, as I repeatedly do in this very play. Praed, the sentimental artist (fool that I was not to make him a theatre critic instead of an architect!) burlesques them by expecting all through the piece that the feelings of others will be logically deducible from their family relationships and from his "conventionally unconventional" social code. The sarcasm is lost on the critics: they, saturated with the same logic, only think him the sole sensible person on the stage. Thus it comes about that the more completely the dramatist is emancipated from the illusion that men and women are primarily reasonable beings, and the more powerfully he insists on the ruthless indifference of their great dramatic antagonist, the external world, to their whims and emotions, the surer he is to be denounced as blind to the very distinction on which his whole work is built. Far from ignoring idiosyncrasy, will, passion, impulse, whim, as factors in human action, I have placed them so nakedly on the stage that the elderly citizen, accustomed to see them clothed with the veil of manufactured logic about duty, and to disguise even his own impulses from himself in this way, finds the picture as unnatural as Carlyle's suggested painting of parliament sitting without its clothes.

I now come to those critics who, intellectually baffled by the problem in Mrs. Warren's Profession, have made a virtue of running away from it. I will illustrate their method by quotation from Dickens, taken from the fifth chapter of Our Mutual Friend:

"Hem!" began Wegg. "This, Mr. Boffin and Lady, is the first chapter of the first wollume of the Decline and Fall off——" here he looked hard at the book, and stopped.

"What's the matter, Wegg?"

"Why, it comes into my mind, do you know, sir," said Wegg with an air of insinuating frankness (having first again looked hard at the book), "that you made a little mistake this morning, which I had meant to set you right in; only something put it out of my head. I think you said Rooshan Empire, sir?"

"It is Rooshan; ain't it, Wegg?"

"No, sir. Roman. Roman."

"What's the difference, Wegg?"

"The difference, sir?" Mr. Wegg was faltering and in danger of breaking down, when a bright thought flashed upon him. "The difference, sir? There you place me in a difficulty, Mr. Boffin. Suffice it to observe, that the difference is best postponed to some other occasion when Mrs. Boffin does not honor us with her company. In Mrs. Boffin's presence, sir, we had better drop it."

Mr. Wegg thus came out of his disadvantage with quite a chivalrous air, and not only that, but by dint of repeating with a manly delicacy, "In Mrs. Boffin's presence, sir, we had better drop it!" turned the disadvantage on Boffin, who felt that he had committed himself in a very painful manner.

I am willing to let Mr. Wegg drop it on these terms, provided I am allowed to mention here that Mrs. Warren's Profession is a play for women; that it was written for women; that it has been performed and produced mainly through the determination of women that it should be performed and produced; that the enthusiasm of women made its first performance excitingly successful; and that not one of these women had any inducement to support it except their belief in the timeliness and the power of the lesson the play teaches. Those who were "surprised to see ladies present" were men; and when they proceeded to explain that the journals they represented could not possibly demoralize the public by describing such a play, their editors cruelly devoted the space saved by their delicacy to an elaborate and respectful account of the progress of a young lord's attempt to break the bank at Monte Carlo. A few days sooner Mrs. Warren would have been crowded out of their papers by an exceptionally abominable police case. I do not suggest that the police case should have been suppressed; but neither do I believe that regard for public morality had anything to do with their failure to grapple with the performance by the Stage Society. And, after all, there was no need to fall back on Silas Wegg's subterfuge. Several critics saved the faces of their papers easily enough by the simple expedient of saying all they had to say in the tone of a shocked governess lecturing a naughty child. To them I might plead, in Mrs. Warren's words, "Well, it's only good manners to be ashamed, dearie;" but it surprises me, recollecting as I do the effect produced by Miss Fanny Brough's delivery of that line, that gentlemen who shivered like violets in a zephyr as it swept through them, should so completely miss the full width of its application as to go home and straightway make a public exhibition of mock modesty.

My old Independent Theatre manager, Mr. Grein, besides that reproach to me for shattering his ideals, complains that Mrs. Warren is not wicked enough, and names several romancers who would have clothed her black soul with all the terrors of tragedy. I have no doubt they would; but if you please, my dear Grein, that is just what I did not want to do. Nothing would please our sanctimonious British public more than to throw the whole guilt of Mrs. Warren's profession on Mrs. Warren herself. Now the whole aim of my play is to throw that guilt on the British public itself. You may remember that when you produced my first play, Widowers' Houses, exactly the same misunderstanding arose. When the virtuous young gentleman rose up in wrath against the slum landlord, the slum landlord very effectively shewed him that slums are the product, not of individual Harpagons, but of the indifference of virtuous young gentlemen to the condition of the city they live in, provided they live at the west end of it on money earned by someone else's labor. The notion that prostitution is created by the wickedness of Mrs. Warren is as silly as the notion—prevalent, nevertheless, to some extent in Temperance circles—that drunkenness is created by the wickedness of the publican. Mrs. Warren is not a whit a worse woman than the reputable daughter who cannot endure her. Her indifference to the ultimate social consequences of her means of making money, and her discovery of that means by the ordinary method of taking the line of least resistance to getting it, are too common in English society to call for any special remark. Her vitality, her thrift, her energy, her outspokenness, her wise care of her daughter, and the managing capacity which has enabled her and her sister to climb from the fried fish shop down by the Mint to the establishments of which she boasts, are all high English social virtues. Her defence of herself is so overwhelming that it provokes the St James Gazette to declare that "the tendency of the play is wholly evil" because "it contains one of the boldest and most specious defences of an immoral life for poor women that has ever been penned." Happily the St James Gazette here speaks in its haste. Mrs. Warren's defence of herself is not only bold and specious, but valid and unanswerable. But it is no defence at all of the vice which she organizes. It is no defence of an immoral life to say that the alternative offered by society collectively to poor women is a miserable life, starved, overworked, fetid, ailing, ugly. Though it is quite natural and *right* for Mrs. Warren to choose what is, according to her lights, the least immoral alternative, it is none the less infamous of society to offer such alternatives. For the alternatives offered are not morality and immorality, but two sorts of immorality. The man who cannot see that starvation, overwork, dirt, and disease are as anti-social as prostitution—that they are the vices and crimes of a nation, and not merely its misfortunes—is (to put it as politely as possible) a hopelessly Private Person.

The notion that Mrs. Warren must be a fiend is only an example of the violence and passion which the slightest reference to sex arouses in undisciplined minds, and which makes it seem natural for our lawgivers to punish silly and negligible indecencies with a ferocity unknown in dealing with, for example, ruinous financial swindling. Had my play been titled Mr. Warren's Profession, and Mr. Warren been a bookmaker, nobody would have expected me to make him a villain as well. Yet gambling is a vice, and bookmaking an institution, for which there is absolutely nothing to be said. The moral and economic evil done by trying to get other people's money without working for it (and this is the essence of gambling) is not only enormous but uncompensated. There are no two sides to the question of gambling, no circumstances which force us to tolerate it lest its suppression lead to worse things, no consensus of opinion among responsible classes, such as magistrates and military commanders, that it is a necessity, no Athenian records of gambling made splendid by the talents of its professors, no contention that instead of violating morals it only violates a legal institution which is in many respects oppressive and unnatural, no possible plea that the instinct on which it is founded is a vital one. Prostitution can confuse the issue with all these excuses: gambling has none of them. Consequently, if Mrs. Warren must needs be a demon, a bookmaker must be a cacodemon. Well, does anybody who knows the sporting world really believe that bookmakers are worse than their neighbors? On the contrary, they have to be a good deal better; for in that world nearly everybody whose social rank does not exclude such an occupation would be a bookmaker if he could; but the strength of character for handling large sums of money and for strict settlements and unflinching payment of losses is so rare that successful bookmakers are rare too. It may seem that at least public spirit cannot be one of a bookmaker's virtues; but I can testify from personal experience that excellent public work is done with money subscribed by bookmakers. It is true that there are abysses in bookmaking: for example, welshing. Mr. Grein hints that there are abysses in Mrs. Warren's profession also. So there are in every profession: the error lies in supposing that every member of them sounds these depths. I sit on a public body which prosecutes Mrs. Warren zealously; and I can assure Mr. Grein that she is often leniently dealt with because she has conducted her business "respectably" and held herself above its vilest branches. The degrees in infamy are as numerous and as scrupulously observed as the degrees in the peerage: the moralist's notion that there are depths at which the moral atmosphere ceases is as delusive as the rich man's notion that there are no social jealousies or snobberies among the very poor. No: had I drawn Mrs. Warren as a fiend in human form, the very people who now rebuke me for flattering her would probably be the first to deride me for deducing her character logically from occupation instead of observing it accurately in society.

One critic is so enslaved by this sort of logic that he calls my portraiture of the Reverend Samuel Gardner an attack on religion.

According to this view Subaltern Iago is an attack on the army, Sir John Falstaff an attack on knighthood, and King Claudius an attack on royalty. Here again the clamor for naturalness and human feeling, raised by so many critics when they are confronted by the real thing on the stage, is really a clamor for the most mechanical and superficial sort of logic. The dramatic reason for making the clergyman what Mrs. Warren calls "an old stick-in-the-mud," whose son, in spite of much capacity and charm, is a cynically worthless member of society, is to set up a mordant contrast between him and the woman of infamous profession, with her well brought-up, straightforward, hardworking daughter. The critics who have missed the contrast have doubtless observed often enough that many clergymen are in the Church through no genuine calling, but simply because, in circles which can command preferment, it is the refuge of "the fool of the family"; and that clergymen's sons are often conspicuous reactionists against the restraints imposed on them in childhood by their father's profession. These critics must know, too, from history if not from experience, that women as unscrupulous as Mrs. Warren have distinguished themselves as administrators and rulers, both commercially and politically. But both observation and knowledge are left behind when journalists go to the theatre. Once in their stalls, they assume that it is "natural" for clergymen to be saintly, for soldiers to be heroic, for lawyers to be hard-hearted, for sailors to be simple and generous, for doctors to perform miracles with little bottles, and for Mrs. Warren to be a beast and a demon. All this is not only not natural, but not dramatic. A man's profession only enters into the drama of his life when it comes into conflict with his nature. The result of this conflict is tragic in Mrs. Warren's case, and comic in the clergyman's case (at least we are savage enough to laugh at it); but in both cases it is illogical, and in both cases natural. I repeat, the critics who accuse me of sacrificing nature to logic are so sophisticated by their profession that to them logic is nature, and nature absurdity.

Many friendly critics are too little skilled in social questions and moral discussions to be able to conceive that respectable gentlemen like themselves, who would instantly call the police to remove Mrs. Warren if she ventured to canvass them personally, could possibly be in any way responsible for her proceedings. They remonstrate sincerely, asking me what good such painful exposures can possibly do. They might as well ask what good Lord Shaftesbury did by devoting his life to the exposure of evils (by no means yet remedied) compared to which the worst things brought into view or even into surmise by this play are trifles. The good of mentioning them is that you make people so extremely uncomfortable about them that they finally stop blaming "human nature" for them, and begin to support measures for their reform.

Can anything be more absurd than the copy of The Echo which contains a notice of the performance of my play? It is edited by a gentleman who, having devoted his life to work of the Shaftesbury type, exposes social evils and clamors for their reform in every column except one; and that one is occupied by the declaration of the paper's kindly theatre critic, that the performance left him "wondering what useful purpose the play was intended to serve." The balance has to be redressed by the more fashionable papers, which usually combine capable art criticism with West-End solecism on politics and sociology. It is very noteworthy, however, on comparing the press explosion produced by Mrs. Warren's Profession in 1902 with that produced by Widowers' Houses about ten years earlier, that whereas in 1892 the facts were frantically denied and the persons of the drama flouted as monsters of wickedness, in 1902 the facts are admitted and the characters recognized, though it is suggested that this is exactly why no gentleman should mention them in public. Only one writer has ventured to imply this time that the poverty mentioned by Mrs. Warren has since been quietly relieved, and need not have been dragged back to the footlights. I compliment him on his splendid mendacity, in which he is unsupported, save by a little plea in a theatrical paper which is innocent enough to think that ten guineas a year with board and lodging is an impossibly low wage for a barmaid. It goes on to cite Mr. Charles Booth as having testified that there are many laborers' wives who are happy and contented on eighteen shillings a week. But I can go further than that myself. I have seen an Oxford agricultural laborer's wife looking cheerful on eight shillings a week; but that does not console me for the fact that agriculture in England is a ruined industry. If poverty does not matter as long as it is contented, then crime does not matter as long as it is unscrupulous. The truth is that it is only then that it does matter most desperately. Many persons are more comfortable when they are dirty than when they are clean; but that does not recommend dirt as a national policy.

Here I must for the present break off my arduous work of educating the Press. We shall resume our studies later on; but just now I am tired of playing the preceptor; and the eager thirst of my pupils for improvement does not console me for the slowness of their progress. Besides, I must reserve space to gratify my own vanity and do justice to the six artists who acted my play, by placing on record the hitherto unchronicled success of the first representation. It is not often that an author, after a couple of hours of those rare alternations of excitement and intensely attentive silence which only occur in the theatre when actors and audience are reacting on one another to the utmost, is able to step on the stage and apply the strong word genius to the representation with the certainty of eliciting an instant and overwhelming assent from the audience. That was my good fortune on the afternoon of Sunday, the fifth of January last. I was certainly extremely fortunate in my interpreters in the enterprise, and that not alone in respect of their artistic talent; for had it not been for their superhuman patience, their imperturbable good humor and good fellowship, there could have been no performance. The terror of the Censor's power gave us trouble enough to break up any ordinary commercial enterprise. Managers promised and even engaged their theatres to us after the most explicit warnings that the play was unlicensed, and at the last moment suddenly realized that Mr. Redford had their livelihoods in the hollow of his hand, and backed out. Over and over again the date and place were fixed and the tickets printed, only to be canceled, until at last the desperate and overworked manager of the Stage Society could only laugh, as criminals broken on the wheel used to laugh at the second stroke. We rehearsed under great difficulties. Christmas pieces and plays for the new year were being produced in all directions; and my six actor colleagues were busy people, with engagements in these pieces in addition to their current professional work every night. On several raw winter days stages for rehearsal were unattainable even by the most distinguished applicants; and we shared corridors and saloons with them whilst the stage was given over to children in training for Boxing night. At last we had to rehearse at an hour at which no actor or actress has been out of bed within the memory of man; and we sardonically congratulated one another every morning on our rosy matutinal looks and the improvement wrought by our early rising in our health and characters. And all this, please observe, for a society without treasury or commercial prestige, for a play which was being denounced in advance as unmentionable, for an author without influence at the fashionable theatres! I victoriously challenge the West End managers to get as much done for interested motives, if they can.

Three causes made the production the most notable that has fallen to my lot. First, the veto of the Censor, which put the supporters of the play on their mettle. Second, the chivalry of the Stage Society, which, in spite of my urgent advice to the contrary, and my demonstration of the difficulties, dangers, and expenses the enterprise would cost, put my discouragements to shame and resolved to give battle at all costs to the attempt of the Censorship to suppress the play. Third, the artistic spirit of the actors, who made the play their own and carried it through triumphantly in spite of a series of disappointments and annoyances much more trying to the dramatic temperament than mere difficulties.

The acting, too, required courage and character as well as skill and intelligence. The veto of the Censor introduced quite a novel element of moral responsibility into the undertaking. And the characters were very unusual on the English stage. The younger heroine is, like her mother, an Englishwoman to the backbone, and not, like the heroines of our fashionable drama, a prima donna of Italian origin. Consequently she was sure to be denounced as unnatural and undramatic by the critics. The most vicious man in the play is not in the least a stage villain; indeed, he regards his own moral character with the sincere complacency of a hero of melodrama. The amiable devotee of romance and beauty is shewn at an age which brings out the futilization which these worships are apt to produce if they are made the staple of life instead of the sauce. The attitude of the clever young people to their elders is faithfully represented as one of pitiless ridicule and unsympathetic criticism, and forms a spectacle incredible to those who, when young, were not cleverer than their nearest elders, and painful to those sentimental parents who shrink from the cruelty of youth, which pardons nothing because it knows nothing. In short, the characters and their relations are of a kind that the routineer critic has not yet learned to place; so that their misunderstanding was a foregone conclusion. Nevertheless, there was no hesitation behind the curtain. When it went up at last, a stage much too small for the company was revealed to an auditorium much too small for the audience. But the players, though it was impossible for them to forget their own discomfort, at once made the spectators forget theirs. It certainly was a model audience, responsive from the first line to the last; and it got no less than it deserved in return.

I grieve to add that the second performance, given for the edification of the London Press and of those members of the Stage Society who cannot attend the Sunday performances, was a less inspiriting one than the first. A solid phalanx of theatre-weary journalists in an afternoon humor, most of them committed to irreconcilable disparagement of problem plays, and all of them bound by etiquette to be as undemonstrative as possible, is not exactly the sort of audience that rises at the performers and cures them of the inevitable reaction after an excitingly successful first night. The artist nature is a sensitive and therefore a vindictive one; and masterful players have a way with recalcitrant audiences of rubbing a play into them instead of delighting them with it. I should describe the second performance of Mrs. Warren's Profession, especially as to its earlier stages, as decidedly a rubbed-in one. The rubbing was no doubt salutary; but it must have hurt some of the thinner skins. The charm of the lighter passages fled; and the strong scenes, though they again carried everything before them, yet discharged that duty in a grim fashion, doing execution on the enemy rather than moving them to repentance and confession. Still, to those who had not seen the first performance, the effect was sufficiently impressive; and they had the advantage of witnessing a fresh development in Mrs. Warren, who, artistically jealous, as I took it, of the overwhelming effect of the end of the second act on the previous day, threw herself into the fourth act in quite a new way, and achieved the apparently impossible feat of surpassing herself. The compliments paid to Miss Fanny Brough by the critics, eulogistic as they are, are the compliments of men three-fourths duped as Partridge was duped by Garrick. By much of her acting they were so completely taken in that they did not recognize it as acting at all. Indeed, none of the six players quite escaped this consequence of their own thoroughness. There was a distinct tendency among the less experienced critics to complain of their sentiments and behavior. Naturally, the author does not share that grievance.

PICCARD'S COTTAGE, JANUARY 1902.

MRS. WARREN'S PROFESSION

Mrs. Warren's Profession was performed for the first time in the theatre of the New Lyric Club, London, on the 5th and 6th January 1902, with Madge McIntosh as Vivie, Julius Knight as Praed, Fanny Brough as Mrs. Warren, Charles Goodhart as Crofts, Harley Granville-Barker as Frank, and Cosmo Stuart as the Reverend Samuel Gardner.

ACT I

Summer afternoon in a cottage garden on the eastern slope of a hill a little south of Haslemere in Surrey. Looking up the hill, the cottage is seen in the left hand corner of the garden, with its thatched roof and porch, and a large latticed window to the left of the porch. A paling completely shuts in the garden, except for a gate on the right. The common rises uphill beyond the paling to the sky line. Some folded canvas garden chairs are leaning against the side bench in the porch. A lady's bicycle is propped against the wall, under the window. A little to the right of the porch a hammock is slung from two posts. A big canvas umbrella, stuck in the ground, keeps the sun off the hammock, in which a young lady is reading and making notes, her head towards the cottage and her feet towards the gate. In front of the hammock, and within reach of her hand, is a common kitchen chair, with a pile of serious-looking books and a supply of writing paper on it.

A gentleman walking on the common comes into sight from behind the cottage. He is hardly past middle age, with something of the artist about him, unconventionally but carefully dressed, and clean-shaven except for a moustache, with an eager susceptible face and very amiable and considerate manners. He has silky black hair, with waves of grey and white in it. His eyebrows are white, his moustache black. He seems not certain of his way. He looks over the palings; takes stock of the place; and sees the young lady.

THE GENTLEMAN. [*taking off his hat*] I beg your pardon. Can you direct me to Hindhead View—Mrs. Alison's?
THE YOUNG LADY. [*glancing up from her book*] This is Mrs. Alison's. [*She resumes her work*].

THE GENTLEMAN. Indeed! Perhaps—may I ask are you Miss Vivie Warren?

THE YOUNG LADY. [*sharply, as she turns on her elbow to get a good look at him*] Yes.

THE GENTLEMAN. [*daunted and conciliatory*] I'm afraid I appear intrusive. My name is Praed. [*VIVIE at once throws her books upon the chair, and gets out of the hammock*]. Oh, pray don't let me disturb you.

VIVIE. [*striding to the gate and opening it for him*] Come in, Mr. Praed. [*He comes in*]. Glad to see you. [*She proffers her hand and takes his with a resolute and hearty grip. She is an attractive specimen of the sensible, able, highly-educated young middle-class Englishwoman. Age 22. Prompt, strong, confident, self-possessed. Plain business-like dress, but not dowdy. She wears a chatelaine at her belt, with a fountain pen and a paper knife among its pendants*].

PRAED. Very kind of you indeed, Miss Warren. [*She shuts the gate with a vigorous slam. He passes in to the middle of the garden, exercising his fingers, which are slightly numbed by her greeting*]. Has your mother arrived?

VIVIE. [*quickly, evidently scenting aggression*] Is she coming?

PRAED. [*surprised*] Didn't you expect us?

VIVIE. No.

PRAED. Now, goodness me, I hope I've not mistaken the day. That would be just like me, you know. Your mother arranged that she was to come down from London and that I was to come over from Horsham to be introduced to you.

VIVIE. [*not at all pleased*] Did she? H'm! My mother has rather a trick of taking me by surprise—to see how I behave myself while she's away, I suppose. I fancy I shall take my mother very much by surprise one of these days, if she makes arrangements that concern me without consulting me beforehand. She hasn't come.

PRAED. [*embarrassed*] I'm really very sorry.

VIVIE. [*throwing off her displeasure*] It's not your fault, Mr. Praed, is it? And I'm very glad you've come. You are the only one of my mother's friends I have ever asked her to bring to see me.

PRAED. [*relieved and delighted*] Oh, now this is really very good of you, Miss Warren!

VIVIE. Will you come indoors; or would you rather sit out here and talk?

PRAED. It will be nicer out here, don't you think?

VIVIE. Then I'll go and get you a chair. [*She goes to the porch for a garden chair*].

PRAED. [*following her*] Oh, pray, pray! Allow me. [*He lays hands on the chair*].

VIVIE. [*letting him take it*] Take care of your fingers; they're rather dodgy things, those chairs. [*She goes across to the chair with the books on it; pitches them into the hammock; and brings the chair forward with one swing*].

PRAED. [*who has just unfolded his chair*] Oh, now do let me take that hard chair. I like hard chairs.

VIVIE. So do I. Sit down, Mr. Praed. [*This invitation she gives with a genial peremptoriness, his anxiety to please her clearly striking her as a sign of weakness of character on his part. But he does not immediately obey*].

PRAED. By the way, though, hadn't we better go to the station to meet your mother?

VIVIE. [*coolly*] Why? She knows the way. [*PRAED hesitates, and then sits down in the garden chair, rather disconcerted.*] Do you know, you are just like what I expected. I hope you are disposed to be friends with me.

PRAED. [*again beaming*] Thank you, my dear Miss Warren; thank you. Dear me! I'm so glad your mother hasn't spoilt you!

VIVIE. How?

PRAED. Well, in making you too conventional. You know, my dear Miss Warren, I am a born anarchist. I hate authority. It spoils the relations between parent and child; even between mother and daughter. Now I was always afraid that your mother would strain her authority to make you very conventional. It's such a relief to find that she hasn't.

VIVIE. Oh! have I been behaving unconventionally?

PRAED. Oh no: oh dear no. At least, not conventionally unconventionally, you understand. [*She nods and sits down. He goes on, with a cordial outburst*] But it was so charming of you to say that you were disposed to be friends with me! You modern young ladies are splendid: perfectly splendid!

VIVIE. [*dubiously*] Eh? [watching him with dawning disappointment as to the quality of his brains and character].

PRAED. When I was your age, young men and women were afraid of each other: there was no good fellowship. Nothing real. Only gallantry copied out of novels, and as vulgar and affected as it could be. Maidenly reserve! gentlemanly chivalry! always saying no when you meant yes! simple purgatory for shy and sincere souls.

VIVIE. Yes, I imagine there must have been a frightful waste of time. Especially women's time.

PRAED. Oh, waste of life, waste of everything. But things are improving. Do you know, I have been in a positive state of excitement about meeting you ever since your magnificent achievements at Cambridge: a thing unheard of in my day. It was perfectly splendid, your tieing with the third wrangler. Just the right place, you know. The first wrangler is always a dreamy, morbid fellow, in whom the thing is pushed to the length of a disease.

VIVIE. It doesn't pay. I wouldn't do it again for the same money.

PRAED. [*aghast*] The same money!

VIVIE. Yes. Fifty pounds. Perhaps you don't know how it was. Mrs. Latham, my tutor at Newnham, told my mother that I could distinguish myself in the mathematical tripos if I went in for it in earnest. The papers were full just then of Phillipa Summers beating the senior wrangler. You remember about it, and nothing would please my mother but that I should do the same thing. I said flatly that it was not worth my while to face the grind since I was not going in for teaching; but I offered to try for fourth wrangler or thereabouts for fifty pounds. She closed with me at that, after a little grumbling; and I was better than my bargain. But I wouldn't do it again for that. Two hundred pounds would have been nearer the mark.

PRAED. [*much damped*] Lord bless me! That's a very practical way of looking at it.

VIVIE. Did you expect to find me an unpractical person?

PRAED. But surely it's practical to consider not only the work these honors cost, but also the culture they bring.

VIVIE. Culture! My dear Mr. Praed: do you know what the mathematical tripos means? It means grind, grind, grind for six to eight hours a day at mathematics, and nothing but mathematics. I'm supposed to know something about science; but I know nothing except the mathematics it involves. I can make calculations for engineers, electricians, insurance companies, and so on; but I know next to nothing about engineering or electricity or insurance. I don't even know arithmetic well. Outside mathematics, lawn-tennis, eating, sleeping, cycling, and walking, I'm a more ignorant barbarian than any woman could possibly be who hadn't gone in for the tripos.

PRAED. [*revolted*] What a monstrous, wicked, rascally system! I knew it! I felt at once that it meant destroying all that makes womanhood beautiful!

VIVIE. I don't object to it on that score in the least. I shall turn it to very good account, I assure you.

PRAED. Pooh! In what way?

VIVIE. I shall set up chambers in the City, and work at actuarial calculations and conveyancing. Under cover of that I shall do some law, with one eye on the Stock Exchange all the time. I've come down here by myself to read law: not for a holiday, as my mother imagines. I hate holidays.

PRAED. You make my blood run cold. Are you to have no romance, no beauty in your life?

VIVIE. I don't care for either, I assure you.

PRAED. You can't mean that.

VIVIE. Oh yes I do. I like working and getting paid for it. When I'm tired of working, I like a comfortable chair, a cigar, a little whisky, and a novel with a good detective story in it.

PRAED. [*in a frenzy of repudiation*] I don't believe it. I am an artist; and I can't believe it: I refuse to believe it. It's only that you haven't discovered yet what a wonderful world art can open up to you.

VIVIE. Yes I have. Last May I spent six weeks in London with Honoria Fraser. Mamma thought we were doing a round of sightseeing together; but I was really at Honoria's chambers in Chancery Lane every day, working away at actuarial calculations for her, and helping her as well as a greenhorn could. In the evenings we smoked and talked, and never dreamt of going out except for exercise. And I never enjoyed myself more in my life. I cleared all my expenses and got initiated into the business without a fee in the bargain.

PRAED. But bless my heart and soul, Miss Warren, do you call that discovering art?

VIVIE. Wait a bit. That wasn't the beginning. I went up to town on an invitation from some artistic people in Fitzjohn's Avenue: one of the girls was a Newnham chum. They took me to the National Gallery, to the Opera, and to a concert where the band played all the evening: Beethoven and Wagner and so on. I wouldn't go through that experience again for anything you could offer me. I held out for civility's sake until the third day; and then I said, plump out, that I couldn't stand any more of it, and went off to Chancery Lane. N o w you know the sort of perfectly splendid modern young lady I am. How do you think I shall get on with my mother?

PRAED. [*startled*] Well, I hope—er—

VIVIE. It's not so much what you hope as what you believe, that I want to know.

PRAED. Well, frankly, I am afraid your mother will be a little disappointed. Not from any shortcoming on your part, you know: I don't mean that. But you are so different from her ideal.

VIVIE. What is her ideal like?

PRAED. Well, you must have observed, Miss Warren, that people who are dissatisfied with their own bringing-up generally think that the world would be all right if everybody were to be brought up quite differently. Now your mother's life has been—er—I suppose you know—

VIVIE. I know nothing. [*PRAED is appalled. His consternation grows as she continues.*] That's exactly my difficulty. You forget, Mr. Praed, that I hardly know my mother. Since I was a child I have lived in England, at school or at college, or with people paid to take charge of me. I have been boarded out all my life; and my mother has lived in Brussels or Vienna and never let me go to her. I only see her when she visits England for a few days. I don't complain: it's been very pleasant; for people have been very good to me; and there has always been plenty of money to make things smooth. But don't imagine I know anything about my mother. I know far less than you do.

PRAED. [*very ill at ease*] In that case—[*He stops, quite at a loss. Then, with a forced attempt at gaiety*] But what nonsense we are talking! Of course you and your mother will get on capitally. [*He rises, and looks abroad at the view*]. What a charming little place you have here!

VIVIE. [*unmoved*] If you think you are doing anything but confirming my worst suspicions by changing the subject like that, you must take me for a much greater fool than I hope I am.

PRAED. Your worst suspicions! Oh, pray don't say that. Now don't.

VIVIE Why won't my mother's life bear being talked about?

PRAED. Pray think, Miss Vivie. It is natural that I should have a certain delicacy in talking to my old friend's daughter about her behind her back. You will have plenty of opportunity of talking to her about it when she comes. [*Anxiously.*] I wonder what is keeping her.

VIVIE. No: she won't talk about it either. [*Rising*] However, I daresay you have good reasons for telling me nothing. Only, mind this, Mr.

Praed, I expect there will be a battle royal when my mother hears of my Chancery Lane project.

PRAED. [*ruefully*] I'm afraid there will.

VIVIE. Well, I shall win because I want nothing but my fare to London to start there to-morrow earning my own living by devilling for Honoria. Besides, I have no mysteries to keep up; and it seems she has. I shall use that advantage over her if necessary.

PRAED. [*greatly shocked*] Oh no! No, pray. You'd not do such a thing.

VIVIE. Then tell me why not.

PRAED. I really cannot. I appeal to your good feeling. [*She smiles at his sentimentality*]. Besides, you may be too bold. Your mother is not to be trifled with when she's angry.

VIVIE. You can't frighten me, Mr. Praed. In that month at Chancery Lane I had opportunities of taking the measure of one or two women v e r y like my mother. You may back me to win. But if I hit harder in my ignorance than I need, remember it is you who refuse to enlighten me. Now, let us drop the subject. [*She takes her chair and replaces it near the hammock with the same vigorous swing as before*].

PRAED. [*taking a desperate resolution*] One word, Miss Warren. I had better tell you. It's very difficult; but—

[*MRS. WARREN and SIR GEORGE CROFTS arrive at the gate. MRS. WARREN is between 40 and 50, formerly pretty, showily dressed in a brilliant hat and a gay blouse fitting tightly over her bust and flanked by fashionable sleeves. Rather spoilt and domineering, and decidedly vulgar, but, on the whole, a genial and fairly presentable old blackguard of a woman.*

CROFTS is a tall powerfully-built man of about 50, fashionably dressed in the style of a young man. Nasal voice, reedier than might be expected from his strong frame. Clean-shaven bulldog jaws, large flat ears, and thick neck: gentlemanly combination of the most brutal types of city man, sporting man, and man about town.]

VIVIE. Here they are. [*Coming to them as they enter the garden*] How do, mater? Mr. Praed's been here this half hour, waiting for you.

MRS. WARREN. Well, if you've been waiting, Praddy, it's your own fault: I thought you'd have had the gumption to know I was coming by the 3.10 train. Vivie: put your hat on, dear: you'll get sunburnt. Oh, I forgot to introduce you. Sir George Crofts: my little Vivie.

[*CROFTS advances to VIVIE with his most courtly manner. She nods, but makes no motion to shake hands.*]

CROFTS. May I shake hands with a young lady whom I have known by reputation very long as the daughter of one of my oldest friends?

VIVIE. [*who has been looking him up and down sharply*] If you like. [*She takes his tenderly proffered hand and gives it a squeeze that makes him open his eyes; then turns away, and says to her mother*] Will you come in, or shall I get a couple more chairs? [*She goes into the porch for the chairs*].

MRS. WARREN. Well, George, what do you think of her?

CROFTS. [*ruefully*] She has a powerful fist. Did you shake hands with her, Praed?

PRAED. Yes: it will pass off presently.

CROFTS. I hope so. [*VIVIE reappears with two more chairs. He hurries to her assistance*]. Allow me.

MRS. WARREN. [*patronizingly*] Let Sir George help you with the chairs, dear.

VIVIE. [pitching them into his arms] Here you are. [*She dusts her hands and turns to MRS. WARREN*]. You'd like some tea, wouldn't you?

MRS. WARREN. [*sitting in PRAED's chair and fanning herself*] I'm dying for a drop to drink.

VIVIE. I'll see about it. [*She goes into the cottage. SIR GEORGE has by this time managed to unfold a chair and plant it by MRS. WARREN, on her left. He throws the other on the grass and sits down, looking dejected and rather foolish, with the handle of his stick in his mouth. PRAED, still very uneasy, fidgets around the garden on their right.*]

MRS. WARREN. [*to PRAED, looking at CROFTS*] Just look at him, Praddy: he looks cheerful, don't he? He's been worrying my life out these three years to have that little girl of mine shewn to him; and now that I've done it, he's quite out of countenance. [*Briskly*] Come! sit up, George; and take your stick out of your mouth. [*CROFTS sulkily obeys*].

PRAED. I think, you know—if you don't mind my saying so—that we had better get out of the habit of thinking of her as a little girl. You see she has really distinguished herself; and I'm not sure, from what I have seen of her, that she is not older than any of us.

MRS. WARREN. [*greatly amused*] Only listen to him, George! Older than any of us! Well she has been stuffing you nicely with her importance.

PRAED. But young people are particularly sensitive about being treated in that way.

MRS. WARREN. Yes; and young people have to get all that nonsense taken out of them, and good deal more besides. Don't you interfere, Praddy: I know how to treat my own child as well as you do. [*PRAED, with a grave shake of his head, walks up the garden with his hands behind his back. MRS. WARREN pretends to laugh, but looks after him with perceptible concern. Then, she whispers to CROFTS*] Whats the matter with him? What does he take it like that for?

CROFTS. [*morosely*] You're afraid of Praed.

MRS. WARREN. What! Me! Afraid of dear old Praddy! Why, a fly wouldn't be afraid of him.

CROFTS. You're afraid of him.

MRS. WARREN. [*angry*] I'll trouble you to mind your own business, and not try any of your sulks on me. I'm not afraid of y o u, anyhow. If you can't make yourself agreeable, you'd better go home. [*She gets up, and, turning her back on him, finds herself face to face with PRAED*]. Come, Praddy, I know it was only your tender-heartedness. You're afraid I'll bully her.

PRAED. My dear Kitty: you think I'm offended. Don't imagine that: pray don't. But you know I often notice things that escape you; and though you never take my advice, you sometimes admit afterwards that you ought to have taken it.

MRS. WARREN. Well, what do you notice now?

PRAED. Only that Vivie is a grown woman. Pray, Kitty, treat her with every respect.

MRS. WARREN. [*with genuine amazement*] Respect! Treat my own daughter with respect! What next, pray!

VIVIE. [appearing at the cottage door and calling to Mrs. Warren] Mother: will you come to my room before tea?

MRS. WARREN. Yes, dearie. [*She laughs indulgently at PRAED'S gravity, and pats him on the cheek as she passes him on her way to the porch*]. Don't be cross, Praddy. [*She follows VIVIE into the cottage*].

CROFTS. [*furtively*] I say, Praed.

PRAED. Yes.

CROFTS. I want to ask you a rather particular question.

PRAED. Certainly. [*He takes MRS. WARREN'S chair and sits close to CROFTS*].

CROFTS. That's right: they might hear us from the window. Look here: did Kitty every tell you who that girl's father is?

PRAED. Never.

CROFTS. Have you any suspicion of who it might be?

PRAED. None.

CROFTS. [*not believing him*] I know, of course, that you perhaps might feel bound not to tell if she had said anything to you. But it's very awkward to be uncertain about it now that we shall be meeting the girl every day. We don't exactly know how we ought to feel towards her.

PRAED. What difference can that make? We take her on her own merits. What does it matter who her father was?

CROFTS. [*suspiciously*] Then you know who he was?

PRAED. [*with a touch of temper*] I said no just now. Did you not hear me?

CROFTS. Look here, Praed. I ask you as a particular favor. If you do know [*movement of protest from PRAED*]—I only say, if you know, you might at least set my mind at rest about her. The fact is, I fell attracted toward her. . Oh, don't be alarmed: it's quite an innocent feeling. That's what puzzles me about it. Why, for all I know, I might be her father.

PRAED. You! Impossible!

CROFTS. [*catching him up cunningly*] You know for certain that I'm not?

PRAED. I know nothing about it, I tell you, any more than you. But really, Crofts—oh no, it's out of the question. There's not the least resemblance.

CROFTS. As to that, there's no resemblance between her and her mother that I can see. I suppose she's not y o u r daughter, is she?

PRAED. [*rising indignantly*] Really, Crofts—!

CROFTS. No offence, Praed. Quite allowable as between two men of the world.

PRAED. [*He meets the question with an indignant stare; then recovers himself with an effort and speaking gently and gravely*] Now listen to me, my dear Crofts. I have nothing to do with that side of Mrs. Warren's life, and never had. She has never spoken to me about it; and of course I have never spoken to her about it. Your delicacy will tell you that a handsome woman needs some friends who are not—well, not on that footing with her. The effect of her own beauty would become a torment to her if she could not escape from it occasionally. You are probably on much more confidential terms with Kitty than I am. Surely you can ask her the question yourself.

CROFTS. [*rising impatiently*] I have asked her, often enough. But she's so determined to keep the child all to herself that she would deny that it ever had a father if she could. [*Rising*] I'm thoroughly uncomfortable about it, Praed.

PRAED. [*rising also*] Well, as you are, at all events, old enough to be her father, I don't mind agreeing that we both regard Miss Vivie in a parental way, as a young girl who we are bound to protect and help. What do you say?

CROFTS. [*aggressively*] I'm no older than you, if you come to that.

PRAED. Yes you are, my dear fellow: you were born old. I was born a boy: I've never been able to feel the assurance of a grown-up man in my life.

MRS. WARREN. [*calling from within the cottage*] Prad-dee! George! Tea-ea-ea-ea!

CROFTS. [*hastily*] She's calling us. [*He hurries in. PRAED shakes his head bodingly, and is following CROFTS when he is hailed by a young gentleman who has just appeared on the common, and is making for the gate. He is pleasant, pretty, smartly dressed, cleverly good-for-nothing, not long turned 20, with a charming voice and agreeably disrespectful manners. He carries a light sporting magazine rifle.*]

THE YOUNG GENTLEMAN. Hallo! Praed!

PRAED. Why, Frank Gardner! [*FRANK comes in and shakes hands cordially*]. What on earth are you doing here?

FRANK. Staying with my father.

PRAED. The Roman father?

FRANK. He's rector here. I'm living with my people this autumn for the sake of economy. Things came to a crisis in July: the Roman father had to pay my debts. He's stony broke in consequence; and so am I. What are you up to in these parts? do you know the people here?

PRAED. Yes: I'm spending the day with a Miss Warren.

FRANK. [*enthusiastically*] What! Do you know Vivie? Isn't she a jolly girl? I'm teaching her to shoot with this [*putting down the rifle*]. I'm so glad she knows you: you're just the sort of fellow she ought to know. [*He smiles, and raises the charming voice almost to a singing tone as he exclaims*] It's e v e r so jolly to find you here, Praed.

PRAED. I'm an old friend of her mother. Mrs. Warren brought me over to make her daughter's acquaintance.

FRANK. The mother! Is she here?

PRAED. Yes: inside, at tea.

MRS. WARREN. [*calling from within*] Prad-dee-ee-ee-eee! The tea-cake'll be cold.

PRAED. [*calling*] Yes, Mrs. Warren. In a moment. I've just met a friend here.

MRS. WARREN. A what?

PRAED. [*louder*] A friend.

MRS. WARREN. Bring him in.

PRAED. All right. [*To FRANK*] Will you accept the invitation?

FRANK. [*incredulous, but immensely amused*] Is that Vivie's mother?

PRAED. Yes.

FRANK. By Jove! What a lark! Do you think she'll like me?

PRAED. I've no doubt you'll make yourself popular, as usual. Come in
and try [*moving towards the house*].

FRANK. Stop a bit. [*Seriously*] I want to take you into my confidence.

PRAED. Pray don't. It's only some fresh folly, like the barmaid at
Redhill.

FRANK. It's ever so much more serious than that. You say you've only
just met Vivie for the first time?

PRAED. Yes.

FRANK. [*rhapsodically*] Then you can have no idea what a girl she is.
Such character! Such sense! And her cleverness! Oh, my eye,
Praed, but I can tell you she is clever! And—need I add?—she
loves me.

CROFTS. [*putting his head out of the window*] I say, Praed: what are
you about? Do come along. [*He disappears*].

FRANK. Hallo! Sort of chap that would take a prize at a dog show,
ain't he? Who's he?

PRAED. Sir George Crofts, an old friend of Mrs. Warren's. I think we
had better come in.

[*On their way to the porch they are interrupted by a call from the
gate. Turning, they see an elderly clergyman looking over it.*]

THE CLERGYMAN. [*calling*] Frank!

FRANK. Hallo! [*To PRAED*] The Roman father. [*To the clergyman*]
Yes, gov'nor: all right: presently. [*To PRAED*] Look here, Praed:
you'd better go in to tea. I'll join you directly.

PRAED. Very good. [*He goes into the cottage. The clergyman remains
outside the gate, with his hands on the top of it. The REV.
SAMUEL GARDNER, a beneficed clergyman of the Established
Church, is over 50. Externally he is pretentious, booming, noisy,
important. Really he is that obsolescent phenomenon the fool of the
family dumped on the Church by his father the patron, clamorously
asserting himself as father and clergyman without being able to
command respect in either capacity.*]

REV. S. Well, sir. Who are your friends here, if I may ask?

FRANK. Oh, it's all right, gov'nor! Come in.

REV. S. No, sir; not until I know whose garden I am entering.

FRANK. It's all right. It's Miss Warren's.

REV. S. I have not seen her at church since she came.

FRANK. Of course not: she's a third wrangler. Ever so intellectual. Took a higher degree than you did; so why should she go to hear you preach?

REV. S. Don't be disrespectful, sir.

FRANK. Oh, it don't matter: nobody hears us. Come in. [He opens the gate, unceremoniously pulling his father with it into the garden]. I want to introduce you to her. Do you remember the advice you gave me last July, gov'nor?

REV. S. [*severely*] Yes. I advised you to conquer your idleness and flippancy, and to work your way into an honorable profession and live on it and not upon me.

FRANK. No: that's what you thought of afterwards. What you actually said was that since I had neither brains nor money, I'd better turn my good looks to account by marrying someone with both. Well, look here. Miss Warren has brains: you can't deny that.

REV. S. Brains are not everything.

FRANK. No, of course not: there's the money—

REV. S. [*interrupting him austerely*] I was not thinking of money, sir. I was speaking of higher things. Social position, for instance.

FRANK. I don't care a rap about that.

REV. S. But I do, sir.

FRANK. Well, nobody wants y o u to marry her. Anyhow, she has what amounts to a high Cambridge degree; and she seems to have as much money as she wants.

REV. S. [*sinking into a feeble vein of humor*] I greatly doubt whether she has as much money as y o u will want.

FRANK. Oh, come: I haven't been so very extravagant. I live ever so quietly; I don't drink; I don't bet much; and I never go regularly to the razzle-dazzle as you did when you were my age.

REV. S. [*booming hollowly*] Silence, sir.

FRANK. Well, you told me yourself, when I was making every such an ass of myself about the barmaid at Redhill, that you once offered a woman fifty pounds for the letters you wrote to her when—

REV. S. [*terrified*] Sh-sh-sh, Frank, for Heaven's sake! [*He looks round apprehensively Seeing no one within earshot he plucks up courage to boom again, but more subduedly*]. You are taking an ungentlemanly advantage of what I confided to you for your own good, to save you from an error you would have repented all your life long. Take warning by your father's follies, sir; and don't make them an excuse for your own.

FRANK. Did you ever hear the story of the Duke of Wellington and his letters?

REV. S. No, sir; and I don't want to hear it.

FRANK. The old Iron Duke didn't throw away fifty pounds: not he. He just wrote: "Dear Jenny: publish and be damned! Yours affectionately, Wellington." That's what you should have done.

REV. S. [*piteously*] Frank, my boy: when I wrote those letters I put myself into that woman's power. When I told you about them I put myself, to some extent, I am sorry to say, in your power. She refused my money with these words, which I shall never forget. "Knowledge is power" she said; "and I never sell power." That's more than twenty years ago; and she has never made use of her power or caused me a moment's uneasiness. You are behaving worse to me than she did, Frank.

FRANK. Oh yes I dare say! Did you ever preach at her the way you preach at me every day?

REV. S. [*wounded almost to tears*] I leave you, sir. You are incorrigible. [*He turns towards the gate*].

FRANK. [*utterly unmoved*] Tell them I shan't be home to tea, will you, gov'nor, like a good fellow? [*He moves towards the cottage door and is met by PRAED and VIVIE coming out*].

VIVIE. [*to FRANK*] Is that your father, Frank? I do so want to meet him.

FRANK. Certainly. [*Calling after his father*] Gov'nor. You're wanted. [*The parson turns at the gate, fumbling nervously at his hat. PRAED crosses the garden to the opposite side, beaming in anticipation of civilities*]. My father: Miss Warren.

VIVIE. [*going to the clergyman and shaking his hand*] Very glad to see you here, Mr. Gardner. [*Calling to the cottage*] Mother: come along: you're wanted.

[*MRS. WARREN appears on the threshold, and is immediately transfixed, recognizing the clergyman.*]

VIVIE. [*continuing*] Let me introduce—

MRS. WARREN. [*swooping on the Reverend Samuel*] Why it's Sam Gardner, gone into the Church! Well, I never! Don't you know us, Sam? This is George Crofts, as large as life and twice as natural. Don't you remember me?

REV. S. [*very red*] I really—er—

MRS. WARREN. Of course you do. Why, I have a whole album of your letters still: I came across them only the other day.

REV. S. [*miserably confused*] Miss Vavasour, I believe.

MRS. WARREN. [*correcting him quickly in a loud whisper*] Tch!
Nonsense! Mrs. Warren: don't you see my daughter there?

ACT II

Inside the cottage after nightfall. Looking eastward from within instead of westward from without, the latticed window, with its curtains drawn, is now seen in the middle of the front wall of the cottage, with the porch door to the left of it. In the left-hand side wall is the door leading to the kitchen. Farther back against the same wall is a dresser with a candle and matches on it, and Frank's rifle standing beside them, with the barrel resting in the plate-rack. In the centre a table stands with a lighted lamp on it. Vivie's books and writing materials are on a table to the right of the window, against the wall. The fireplace is on the right, with a settle: there is no fire. Two of the chairs are set right and left of the table.

The cottage door opens, shewing a fine starlit night without; and Mrs. Warren, her shoulders wrapped in a shawl borrowed from Vivie, enters, followed by Frank, who throws his cap on the window seat. She has had enough of walking, and gives a gasp of relief as she unpins her hat; takes it off; sticks the pin through the crown; and puts it on the table.

MRS. WARREN. O Lord! I don't know which is the worst of the country, the walking or the sitting at home with nothing to do. I could do with a whisky and soda now very well, if only they had such a things in this place.

FRANK. Perhaps Vivie's got some.

MRS. WARREN. Nonsense! What would a young girl like her be doing with such things! Never mind: it don't matter. I wonder how she passes her time here! I'd a good deal rather be in Vienna.

FRANK. Let me take you there. [*He helps her to take off her shawl, gallantly giving her shoulders a very perceptible squeeze as he does so*].

MRS. WARREN. Get out! I'm beginning to think you're a chip of the old block.

FRANK. Like the gov'nor, eh?

MRS. WARREN. Never you mind. What do you know about such things? You're only a boy.

FRANK. Do come to Vienna with me? It'd be ever such larks.

MRS. WARREN. No, thank you. Vienna is no place for you—at least not until you're a little older. [*She nods at him to emphasize this piece of advice. He makes a mock-piteous face, belied by his laughing eyes. She looks at him; then comes back to him*]. Now, look here, little boy [*taking his face in her hands and turning it up to her*]: I know you through and through by your likeness to your father, better than you know yourself. Don't you go taking any silly ideas into your head about me. Do you hear?

FRANK. [*gallantly wooing her with his voice*] Can't help it, my dear Mrs. Warren: it runs in the family. [*She pretends to box his ears; then looks at the pretty laughing upturned face of a moment, tempted. At last she kisses him, and immediately turns away, out of patience with herself.*]

MRS. WARREN. There! I shouldn't have done that. I am wicked. Never you mind, my dear: it's only a motherly kiss. Go and make love to Vivie.

FRANK. So I have.

MRS. WARREN. [*turning on him with a sharp note of alarm in her voice*] What!

FRANK. Vivie and I are ever such chums.

MRS. WARREN. What do you mean? Now see here: I won't have any young scamp tampering with my little girl. Do you hear? I won't have it.

FRANK. [*quite unabashed*] My dear Mrs. Warren: don't you be alarmed. My intentions are honorable: ever so honorable; and your little girl is jolly well able to take care of herself. She don't need looking after half so much as her mother. She ain't so handsome, you know.

MRS. WARREN. [*taken aback by his assurance*] Well, you have got a nice healthy two inches of cheek all over you. I don't know where you got it. Not from your father, anyhow.

CROFTS. [*in the garden*] The gipsies, I suppose?

REV. S. [*replying*] The broomsquires are far worse.

MRS. WARREN. [*to FRANK*] S-sh! Remember! you've had your warning. [*CROFTS and the REVEREND SAMUEL GARDNER come in from the garden, the clergyman continuing his conversation as he enters.*]

REV. S. The perjury at the Winchester assizes is deplorable.

MRS. WARREN. Well? what became of you two? And wheres Praddy and Vivie?

CROFTS. [*putting his hat on the settle and his stick in the chimney corner*] They went up the hill. We went to the village. I wanted a drink. [*He sits down on the settle, putting his legs up along the seat*].

MRS. WARREN. Well, she oughtn't to go off like that without telling me. [*To FRANK*] Get your father a chair, Frank: where are your manners? [*FRANK springs up and gracefully offers his father his chair; then takes another from the wall and sits down at the table, in the middle, with his father on his right and MRS. WARREN on his left*]. George: where are you going to stay to-night? You can't stay here. And what's Praddy going to do?

CROFTS. Gardner'll put me up.

MRS. WARREN. Oh, no doubt you've taken care of yourself! But what about Praddy?

CROFTS. Don't know. I suppose he can sleep at the inn.

MRS. WARREN. Haven't you room for him, Sam?

REV. S. Well—er—you see, as rector here, I am not free to do as I like. Er—what is Mr. Praed's social position?

MRS. WARREN. Oh, he's all right: he's an architect. What an old stick-in-the-mud you are, Sam!

FRANK. Yes, it's all right, gov'nor. He built that place down in Wales for the Duke. Caernarvon Castle they call it. You must have heard of it. [*He winks with lightning smartness at MRS. WARREN, and regards his father blandly*].

REV. S. Oh, in that case, of course we shall only be too happy. I suppose he knows the Duke personally.

FRANK. Oh, ever so intimately! We can stick him in Georgina's old room.

MRS. WARREN. Well, that's settled. Now if those two would only come in and let us have supper. They've no right to stay out after dark like this.

CROFTS. [*aggressively*] What harm are they doing you?

MRS. WARREN. Well, harm or not, I don't like it.

FRANK. Better not wait for them, Mrs. Warren. Praed will stay out as long as possible. He has never known before what it is to stray over the heath on a summer night with my Vivie.

CROFTS. [*sitting up in some consternation*] I say, you know! Come!

REV. S. [*rising, startled out of his professional manner into real force and sincerity*] Frank, once and for all, it's out of the question. Mrs. Warren will tell you that it's not to be thought of.

CROFTS. Of course not.

FRANK. [*with enchanting placidity*] Is that so, Mrs. Warren?

MRS. WARREN. [*reflectively*] Well, Sam, I don't know. If the girl wants to get married, no good can come of keeping her unmarried.

REV. S. [*astounded*] But married to him!—your daughter to my son! Only think: it's impossible.

CROFTS. Of course it's impossible. Don't be a fool, Kitty.

MRS. WARREN. [*nettled*] Why not? Isn't my daughter good enough for your son?

REV. S. But surely, my dear Mrs. Warren, you know the reasons—

MRS. WARREN. [*defiantly*] I know no reasons. If you know any, you can tell them to the lad, or to the girl, or to your congregation, if you like.

REV. S. [*collapsing helplessly into his chair*] You know very well that I couldn't tell anyone the reasons. But my boy will believe me when I tell him there a r e reasons.

FRANK. Quite right, Dad: he will. But has your boy's conduct ever been influenced by your reasons?

CROFTS. You can't marry her; and that's all about it. [*He gets up and stands on the hearth, with his back to the fireplace, frowning determinedly*].

MRS. WARREN. [*turning on him sharply*] What have you got to do with it, pray?

FRANK. [*with his prettiest lyrical cadence*] Precisely what I was going to ask, myself, in my own graceful fashion.

CROFTS. [*to MRS. WARREN*] I suppose you don't want to marry the girl to a man younger than herself and without either a profession or twopence to keep her on. Ask Sam, if you don't believe me. [*To the parson*] How much more money are you going to give him?

REV. S. Not another penny. He has had his patrimony; and he spent the last of it in July. [*MRS. WARREN'S face falls*].

CROFTS. [*watching her*] There! I told you. [*He resumes his place on the settle and puts his legs on the seat again, as if the matter were finally disposed of*].

FRANK. [*plaintively*] This is ever so mercenary. Do you suppose Miss Warren's going to marry for money? If we love one another—

MRS. WARREN. Thank you. Your love's a pretty cheap commodity, my lad. If you have no means of keeping a wife, that settles it; you can't have Vivie.

FRANK. [*much amused*] What do y o u say, gov'nor, eh?

REV. S. I agree with Mrs. Warren.

FRANK. And good old Crofts has already expressed his opinion.

CROFTS. [turning angrily on his elbow] Look here: I want none of your cheek.

FRANK. [*pointedly*] I'm e v e r so sorry to surprise you, Crofts; but you allowed yourself the liberty of speaking to me like a father a moment ago. One father is enough, thank you.

CROFTS. [*contemptuously*] Yah! [*He turns away again*].

FRANK. [*rising*] Mrs. Warren: I cannot give my Vivie up, even for your sake.

MRS. WARREN. [*muttering*] Young scamp!

FRANK. [*continuing*] And as you no doubt intend to hold out other prospects to her, I shall lose no time in placing my case before her. [*They stare at him; and he begins to declaim gracefully*]

> He either fears his fate too much,
>   Or his deserts are small,
> That dares not put it to the touch,
>   To gain or lose it all.

[*The cottage doors open whilst he is reciting; and VIVIE and PRAED come in. He breaks off. PRAED puts his hat on the dresser. There is an immediate improvement in the company's behavior. CROFTS takes down his legs from the settle and pulls himself together as PRAED joins him at the fireplace. MRS. WARREN loses her ease of manner and takes refuge in querulousness.*]

MRS. WARREN. Wherever have you been, Vivie?

VIVIE. [*taking off her hat and throwing it carelessly on the table*] On the hill.

MRS. WARREN. Well, you shouldn't go off like that without letting me know. How could I tell what had become of you? And night coming on too!

VIVIE. [*going to the door of the kitchen and opening it, ignoring her mother*] Now, about supper? [*All rise except MRS. WARREN*] We shall be rather crowded in here, I'm afraid.

MRS. WARREN. Did you hear what I said, Vivie?

VIVIE. [*quietly*] Yes, mother. [*Reverting to the supper difficulty*] How many are we? [*Counting*] One, two, three, four, five, six. Well, two will have to wait until the rest are done: Mrs. Alison has only plates and knives for four.

PRAED. Oh, it doesn't matter about me. I—

VIVIE. You have had a long walk and are hungry, Mr. Praed: you shall have your supper at once. I can wait myself. I want one person to wait with me. Frank: are you hungry?

FRANK. Not the least in the world. Completely off my peck, in fact.

MRS. WARREN. [*to CROFTS*] Neither are you, George. You can wait.

CROFTS. Oh, hang it, I've eaten nothing since tea-time. Can't Sam do it?

FRANK. Would you starve my poor father?

REV. S. [*testily*] Allow me to speak for myself, sir. I am perfectly willing to wait.

VIVIE. [*decisively*] There's no need. Only two are wanted. [*She opens the door of the kitchen*]. Will you take my mother in, Mr. Gardner. [*The parson takes MRS. WARREN; and they pass into the kitchen. PRAED and CROFTS follow. All except PRAED clearly disapprove of the arrangement, but do not know how to resist it. VIVIE stands at the door looking in at them*]. Can you squeeze past to that corner, Mr. Praed: it's rather a tight fit. Take care of your coat against the white-wash: that right. Now, are you all comfortable?

PRAED. [*within*] Quite, thank you.

MRS. WARREN. [*within*] Leave the door open, dearie. [*VIVIE frowns; but FRANK checks her with a gesture, and steals to the cottage door, which he softly sets wide open*]. Oh Lor', what a draught! You'd better shut it, dear. [*VIVIE shuts it with a slam, and then, noting with disgust that her mother's hat and shawl are lying about, takes them tidily to the window seat, whilst FRANK noiselessly shuts the cottage door.*]

FRANK. [*exulting*] Aha! Got rid of em. Well, Vivvums: what do you think of my governor?

VIVIE. [*preoccupied and serious*] I've hardly spoken to him. He doesn't strike me as a particularly able person.

FRANK. Well, you know, the old man is not altogether such a fool as he looks. You see, he was shoved into the Church, rather; and in trying to live up to it he makes a much bigger ass of himself than he really is. I don't dislike him as much as you might expect. He means well. How do you think you'll get on with him?

VIVIE. [*rather grimly*] I don't think my future life will be much concerned with him, or with any of that old circle of my mother's, except perhaps Praed. [*She sits down on the settle*] What do you think of my mother?

FRANK. Really and truly?

VIVIE. Yes, really and truly.

FRANK. Well, she's ever so jolly. But she's rather a caution, isn't she? And Crofts! Oh, my eye, Crofts! [*He sits beside her*].

VIVIE. What a lot, Frank!

FRANK. What a crew!

VIVIE. [*with intense contempt for them*] If I thought that I was like that—that I was going to be a waster, shifting along from one meal to another with no purpose, and no character, and no grit in me, I'd open an artery and bleed to death without one moment's hesitation.

FRANK. Oh no, you wouldn't. Why should they take any grind when they can afford not to? I wish I had their luck. No: what I object to is their form. It isn't the thing: it's slovenly, ever so slovenly.

VIVIE. Do you think your form will be any better when you're as old as Crofts, if you don't work?

FRANK. Of course I do. Ever so much better. Vivvums mustn't lecture: her little boy's incorrigible. [*He attempts to take her face caressingly in his hands*].

VIVIE. [*striking his hands down sharply*] Off with you: Vivvums is not in a humor for petting her little boy this evening. [*She rises and comes forward to the other side of the room*].

FRANK. [*following her*] How unkind!

VIVIE. [*stamping at him*] Be serious. I'm serious.

FRANK. Good. Let us talk learnedly, Miss Warren: do you know that all the most advanced thinkers are agreed that half the diseases of modern civilization are due to starvation of the affections of the young. Now, I—

VIVIE. [*cutting him short*] You are very tiresome. [*She opens the inner door*] Have you room for Frank there? He's complaining of starvation.

MRS. WARREN. [*within*] Of course there is [*clatter of knives and glasses as she moves the things on the table*]. Here! there's room now beside me. Come along, Mr. Frank.

FRANK. Her little boy will be ever so even with his Vivvums for this. [*He passes into the kitchen*].

MRS. WARREN. [*within*] Here, Vivie: come on you too, child. You must be famished. [*She enters, followed by CROFTS, who holds the door open with marked deference. She goes out without looking at him; and he shuts the door after her*]. Why George, you can't be done: you've eaten nothing. Is there anything wrong with you?

CROFTS. Oh, all I wanted was a drink. [*He thrusts his hands in his pockets, and begins prowling about the room, restless and sulky*].

MRS. WARREN. Well, I like enough to eat. But a little of that cold beef and cheese and lettuce goes a long way. [*With a sigh of only half repletion she sits down lazily on the settle*].

CROFTS. What do you go encouraging that young pup for?

MRS. WARREN. [*on the alert at once*] Now see here, George: what are you up to about that girl? I've been watching your way of looking at her. Remember: I know you and what your looks mean.

CROFTS. There's no harm in looking at her, is there?

MRS. WARREN. I'd put you out and pack you back to London pretty soon if I saw any of your nonsense. My girl's little finger is more to me than your whole body and soul. [*CROFTS receives this with a sneering grin. MRS. WARREN, flushing a little at her failure to impose on him in the character of a theatrically devoted mother, adds in a lower key*] Make your mind easy: the young pup has no more chance than you have.

CROFTS. Mayn't a man take an interest in a girl?

MRS. WARREN. Not a man like you.

CROFTS. How old is she?

MRS. WARREN. Never you mind how old she is.

CROFTS. Why do you make such a secret of it?

MRS. WARREN. Because I choose.

CROFTS. Well, I'm not fifty yet; and my property is as good as it ever was—

MRS. WARREN. [*interrupting him*] Yes; because you're as stingy as you're vicious.

CROFTS. [*continuing*] And a baronet isn't to be picked up every day. No other man in my position would put up with you for a mother-in-law. Why shouldn't she marry me?

MRS. WARREN. You!

CROFTS. We three could live together quite comfortably. I'd die before her and leave her a bouncing widow with plenty of money. Why not? It's been growing in my mind all the time I've been walking with that fool inside there.

MRS. WARREN. [*revolted*] Yes; it's the sort of thing that would grow in your mind. [*He halts in his prowling; and the two look at one another, she steadfastly, with a sort of awe behind her contemptuous disgust: he stealthily, with a carnal gleam in his eye and a loose grin.*]

CROFTS. [*suddenly becoming anxious and urgent as he sees no sign of sympathy in her*] Look here, Kitty: you're a sensible woman: you needn't put on any moral airs. I'll ask no more questions; and you need answer none. I'll settle the whole property on her; and if you want a cheque for yourself on the wedding day, you can name any figure you like—in reason.

MRS. WARREN. So it's come to that with you, George, like all the other worn-out old creatures!

CROFTS. [*savagely*] Damn you! [*Before she can retort the door of the kitchen is opened; and the voices of the others are heard returning. CROFTS, unable to recover his presence of mind, hurries out of the cottage. The clergyman appears at the kitchen door.*]

REV. S. [*looking round*] Where is Sir George?

MRS. WARREN. Gone out to have a pipe. [*The clergyman takes his hat from the table, and joins MRS. WARREN at the fireside. Meanwhile, VIVIE comes in, followed by FRANK, who collapses into the nearest chair with an air of extreme exhaustion. MRS. WARREN looks round at VIVIE and says, with her affectation of maternal patronage even more forced than usual*] Well, dearie: have you had a good supper?

VIVIE. You know what Mrs. Alison's suppers are. [She turns to FRANK and pets him] Poor Frank! was all the beef gone? did it get nothing but bread and cheese and ginger beer? [*Seriously, as if she had done quite enough trifling for one evening*] Her butter is really awful. I must get some down from the stores.

FRANK. Do, in Heaven's name!

[*VIVIE goes to the writing-table and makes a memorandum to order the butter. PRAED comes in from the kitchen, putting up his handkerchief, which he has been using as a napkin.*]

REV. S. Frank, my boy: it is time for us to be thinking of home. Your mother does not know yet that we have visitors.

PRAED. I'm afraid we're giving trouble.

FRANK. [*rising*] Not the least in the world: my mother will be delighted to see you. She's a genuinely intellectual artistic woman; and she sees nobody here from one year's end to another except the gov'nor; so you can imagine how jolly dull it pans out for her. [*To his father*] Y o u r e not intellectual or artistic: are you pater? So take Praed home at once; and I'll stay here and entertain Mrs. Warren. You'll pick up Crofts in the garden. He'll be excellent company for the bull-pup.

PRAED. [*taking his hat from the dresser, and coming close to FRANK*] Come with us, Frank. Mrs. Warren has not seen Miss Vivie for a long time; and we have prevented them from having a moment together yet.

FRANK. [*quite softened, and looking at PRAED with romantic admiration*] Of course. I forgot. Ever so thanks for reminding me. Perfect gentleman, Praddy. Always were. My ideal through life. [*He rises to go, but pauses a moment between the two older men, and puts his hand on PRAED'S shoulder*]. Ah, if you had only been my father instead of this unworthy old man! [*He puts his other hand on his father's shoulder*].

REV. S. [*blustering*] Silence, sir, silence: you are profane.

MRS. WARREN. [*laughing heartily*] You should keep him in better order, Sam. Good-night. Here: take George his hat and stick with my compliments.

REV. S. [*taking them*] Good-night. [*They shake hands. As he passes VIVIE he shakes hands with her also and bids her good-night. Then, in booming command, to FRANK*] Come along, sir, at once. [*He goes out. Meanwhile FRANK has taken his cap from the dresser and his rifle from the rack. PRAED shakes hands with MRS. WARREN and VIVIE and goes out, MRS. WARREN accompanying him idly to the door, and looking out after him as he goes across the garden. FRANK silently begs a kiss from VIVIE; but she, dismissing him with a stern glance, takes a couple of books and some paper form the writing-table, and sits down with them at the middle, so as to have the benefit of the lamp.]*].

FRANK. [*at the door, taking MRS. WARREN'S hand*] Good-night, dear Mrs. Warren. [*He kisses her hand. She snatches it away, her lips tightening, and looks more than half disposed to box his ears. He laughs mischievously and runs off, clapping-to the door behind him*].

MRS. WARREN. [*resigning herself to an evening of boredom now that the men are gone*] Did you ever in your life hear anyone rattle on so? Isn't he a tease? [*She sits at the table*]. Now that I think of it, dearie, don't you go encouraging him. I'm sure he's a regular good-for-nothing.

VIVIE. [*rising to fetch more books*] I'm afraid so. Poor Frank! I shall have to get rid of him; but I shall feel sorry for him, though he's not worth it. That man Crofts does not seem to me to be good for much either: is he? [*She throws the books on the table rather roughly*].

MRS. WARREN. [*galled by VIVIE's indifference*] What do you know of men, child, to talk that way of them? You'll have to make up your mind to see a good deal of Sir George Crofts, as he's a friend of mine.

VIVIE. [*quite unmoved*] Why? [*She sits down and opens a book*]. Do you expect that we shall be much together? You and I, I mean?

MRS. WARREN. [*staring at her*] Of course: until you're married. You're not going back to college again.

VIVIE. Do you think my way of life would suit you? I doubt it.

MRS. WARREN. Y o u r way of life! What do you mean?

VIVIE. [*cutting a page of her book with the paper knife on her chatelaine*] Has it really never occurred to you, mother, that I have a way of life like other people?

MRS. WARREN. What nonsense is this you're trying to talk? Do you want to shew your independence, now that you're a great little person at school? Don't be a fool, child.

VIVIE. [*indulgently*] That's all you have to say on the subject, is it, mother?

MRS. WARREN. [*puzzled, then angry*] Don't you keep on asking me questions like that. [*Violently*] Hold your tongue. [*VIVIE works on, losing no time, and saying nothing*]. You and your way of life, indeed! What next? [*She looks at VIVIE again. No reply*]. Your way of life will be what I please, so it will. [*Another pause*]. Ive been noticing these airs in you ever since you got that tripos or whatever you call it. If you think I'm going to put up with them, you're mistaken; and the sooner you find it out, the better. [*Muttering*] All I have to say on the subject, indeed! [*Again raising her voice angrily*] Do you know who you're speaking to, Miss?

VIVIE. [*looking across at her without raising her head from her book*] No. Who are you? What are you?

MRS. WARREN. [*rising breathless*] You young imp!

VIVIE. Everybody knows my reputation, my social standing, and the profession I intend to pursue. I know nothing about you. What is that way of life which you invite me to share with you and Sir George Crofts, pray?

MRS. WARREN. Take care. I shall do something I'll be sorry for after, and you too.

VIVIE. [*putting aside her books with cool decision*] Well, let us drop the subject until you are better able to face it. [*Looking critically at her mother*] You want some good walks and a little lawn tennis to set you up. You are shockingly out of condition: you were not able to manage twenty yards uphill today without stopping to pant; and your wrists are mere rolls of fat. Look at mine. [*She holds out her wrists*].

MRS. WARREN. [*after looking at her helplessly, begins to whimper*] Vivie—

VIVIE. [*springing up sharply*] Now pray don't begin to cry. Anything but that. I really cannot stand whimpering. I will go out of the room if you do.

MRS. WARREN. [*piteously*] Oh, my darling, how can you be so hard on me? Have I no rights over you as your mother?

VIVIE. A r e you my mother?

MRS. WARREN. Am I your mother? Oh, Vivie!

VIVIE. Then where are our relatives? my father? our family friends? You claim the rights of a mother: the right to call me fool and child; to speak to me as no woman in authority over me at college dare speak to me; to dictate my way of life; and to force on me the acquaintance of a brute whom anyone can see to be the most vicious sort of London man about town. Before I give myself the trouble to resist such claims, I may as well find out whether they have any real existence.

MRS. WARREN. [*distracted, throwing herself on her knees*] Oh no, no. Stop, stop. I am your mother: I swear it. Oh, you can't mean to turn on me—my own child! it's not natural. You believe me, don't you? Say you believe me.

VIVIE. Who was my father?

MRS. WARREN. You don't know what you're asking. I can't tell you.

VIVIE. [*determinedly*] Oh yes you can, if you like. I have a right to know; and you know very well that I have that right. You can refuse to tell me if you please; but if you do, you will see the last of me tomorrow morning.

MRS. WARREN. Oh, it's too horrible to hear you talk like that. You wouldn't—you couldn't leave me.

VIVIE. [*ruthlessly*] Yes, without a moment's hesitation, if you trifle with me about this. [*Shivering with disgust*] How can I feel sure that I may not have the contaminated blood of that brutal waster in my veins?

MRS. WARREN. No, no. On my oath it's not he, nor any of the rest that you have ever met. I'm certain of that, at least. [*VIVIE's eyes fasten sternly on her mother as the significance of this flashes on her.*]

VIVIE. [*slowly*] You are certain of that, at least. Ah! You mean that that is all you are certain of. [*Thoughtfully*] I see. [*MRS. WARREN buries her face in her hands*]. Don't do that, mother: you know you don't feel it a bit. [*MRS. WARREN takes down her hands and looks up deplorably at VIVIE, who takes out her watch and says*] Well, that is enough for tonight. At what hour would you like breakfast? Is half-past eight too early for you?

MRS. WARREN. [*wildly*] My God, what sort of woman are you?

VIVIE. [*coolly*] The sort the world is mostly made of, I should hope. Otherwise I don't understand how it gets its business done. Come [*taking her mother by the wrist and pulling her up pretty resolutely*]: pull yourself together. That's right.

MRS. WARREN. [*querulously*] You're very rough with me, Vivie.

VIVIE. Nonsense. What about bed? It's past ten.

MRS. WARREN. [*passionately*] What's the use of my going to bed? Do you think I could sleep?

VIVIE. Why not? I shall.

MRS. WARREN. You! you've no heart. [*She suddenly breaks out vehemently in her natural tongue—the dialect of a woman of the people—with all her affectations of maternal authority and conventional manners gone, and an overwhelming inspiration of true conviction and scorn in her*] Oh, I wont bear it: I won't put up with the injustice of it. What right have you to set yourself up above me like this? You boast of what you are to me—to me, who gave you a chance of being what you are. What chance had I? Shame on you for a bad daughter and a stuck-up prude!

VIVIE. [*sitting down with a shrug, no longer confident; for her replies, which have sounded sensible and strong to her so far, now begin to ring rather woodenly and even priggishly against the new tone of her mother*] Don't think for a moment I set myself above you in any way. You attacked me with the conventional authority of a mother: I defended myself with the conventional superiority of a respectable woman. Frankly, I am not going to stand any of your nonsense; and when you drop it I shall not expect you to stand any of mine. I shall always respect your right to your own opinions and your own way of life.

MRS. WARREN. My own opinions and my own way of life! Listen to her talking! Do you think I was brought up like you? able to pick and choose my own way of life? Do you think I did what I did because I liked it, or thought it right, or wouldn't rather have gone to college and been a lady if I'd had the chance?

VIVIE. Everybody has some choice, mother. The poorest girl alive may not be able to choose between being Queen of England or Principal of Newnham; but she can choose between ragpicking and flowerselling, according to her taste. People are always blaming circumstances for what they are. I don't believe in circumstances. The people who get on in this world are the people who get up and look for the circumstances they want, and, if they can't find them, make them.

MRS. WARREN. Oh, it's easy to talk, isn't it? Here! would you like to know what my circumstances were?

VIVIE. Yes: you had better tell me. Won't you sit down?

MRS. WARREN. Oh, I'll sit down: don't you be afraid. [She plants her chair farther forward with brazen energy, and sits down. Vivie is impressed in spite of herself]. D'you know what your gran'mother was?

VIVIE. No.

MRS. WARREN. No, you don't. I do. She called herself a widow and had a fried-fish shop down by the Mint, and kept herself and four daughters out of it. Two of us were sisters: that was me and Liz; and we were both good-looking and well made. I suppose our father was a well-fed man: mother pretended he was a gentleman; but I don't know. The other two were only half sisters: undersized, ugly, starved looking, hard working, honest poor creatures: Liz and I would have half-murdered them if mother hadn't half-murdered us to keep our hands off them. They were the respectable ones. Well, what did they get by their respectability? I'll tell you. One of them worked in a whitelead factory twelve hours a day for nine shillings a week until she died of lead poisoning. She only expected to get her hands a little paralyzed; but she died. The other was always held up to us as a model because she married a Government laborer in the Deptford victualling yard, and kept his room and the three children neat and tidy on eighteen shillings a week—until he took to drink. That was worth being respectable for, wasn't it?

VIVIE. [*now thoughtfully attentive*] Did you and your sister think so?

MRS. WARREN. Liz didn't, I can tell you: she had more spirit. We both went to a church school—that was part of the ladylike airs we gave ourselves to be superior to the children that knew nothing and went nowhere—and we stayed there until Liz went out one night and never came back. I know the schoolmistress thought I'd soon follow her example; for the clergyman was always warning me that Lizzie'd end by jumping off Waterloo Bridge. Poor fool: that was all he knew about it! But I was more afraid of the whitelead factory than I was of the river; and so would you have been in my place. That clergyman got me a situation as a scullery maid in a temperance restaurant where they sent out for anything you liked. Then I was a waitress; and then I went to the bar at Waterloo station: fourteen hours a day serving drinks and washing glasses for four shillings a week and my board. That was considered a great promotion for me. Well, one cold, wretched night, when I was so tired I could hardly keep myself awake, who should come up for a half of Scotch but Lizzie, in a long fur cloak, elegant and comfortable, with a lot of sovereigns in her purse.

VIVIE. [*grimly*] My aunt Lizzie!

MRS. WARREN. Yes; and a very good aunt to have, too. She's living down at Winchester now, close to the cathedral, one of the most respectable ladies there. Chaperones girls at the country ball, if you please. No river for Liz, thank you! You remind me of Liz a little: she was a first-rate business woman—saved money from the beginning—never let herself look too like what she was—never lost her head or threw away a chance. When she saw I'd grown up good-looking she said to me across the bar "What are you doing there, you little fool? wearing out your health and your appearance for other people's profit!" Liz was saving money then to take a house for herself in Brussels; and she thought we two could save faster than one. So she lent me some money and gave me a start; and I saved steadily and first paid her back, and then went into business with her as a partner. Why shouldn't I have done it? The house in Brussels was real high class: a much better place for a woman to be in than the factory where Anne Jane got poisoned. None of the girls were ever treated as I was treated in the scullery of that temperance place, or at the Waterloo bar, or at home. Would you have had me stay in them and become a worn out old drudge before I was forty?

VIVIE. [*intensely interested by this time*] No; but why did you choose that business? Saving money and good management will succeed in any business.

MRS. WARREN. Yes, saving money. But where can a woman get the money to save in any other business? Could y o u save out of four shillings a week and keep yourself dressed as well? Not you. Of course, if you're a plain woman and can't earn anything more; or if you have a turn for music, or the stage, or newspaper-writing: that's different. But neither Liz nor I had any turn for such things at all: all we had was our appearance and our turn for pleasing men. Do you think we were such fools as to let other people trade in our good looks by employing us as shopgirls, or barmaids, or waitresses, when we could trade in them ourselves and get all the profits instead of starvation wages? Not likely.

VIVIE. You were certainly quite justified—from the business point of view.

MRS. WARREN. Yes; or any other point of view. What is any respectable girl brought up to do but to catch some rich man's fancy and get the benefit of his money by marrying him?—as if a marriage ceremony could make any difference in the right or wrong of the thing! Oh, the hypocrisy of the world makes me sick! Liz and I had to work and save and calculate just like other people; elseways we should be as poor as any good-for-nothing drunken waster of a woman that thinks her luck will last for ever. [*With great energy*] I despise such people: they've no character; and if there's a thing I hate in a woman, it's want of character.

VIVIE. Come now, mother: frankly! Isn't it part of what you call character in a woman that she should greatly dislike such a way of making money?

MRS. WARREN. Why, of course. Everybody dislikes having to work and make money; but they have to do it all the same. I'm sure I've often pitied a poor girl, tired out and in low spirits, having to try to please some man that she doesn't care two straws for—some half-drunken fool that thinks he's making himself agreeable when he's teasing and worrying and disgusting a woman so that hardly any money could pay her for putting up with it. But she has to bear with disagreeables and take the rough with the smooth, just like a nurse in a hospital or anyone else. It's not work that any woman would do for pleasure, goodness knows; though to hear the pious people talk you would suppose it was a bed of roses.

VIVIE. Still, you consider it worth while. It pays.

MRS. WARREN. Of course it's worth while to a poor girl, if she can resist temptation and is good-looking and well conducted and sensible. It's far better than any other employment open to her. I always thought that it oughtn't to be. It can't be right, Vivie, that there shouldn't be better opportunities for women. I stick to that: it's wrong. But it's so, right or wrong; and a girl must make the best of it. But of course it's not worth while for a lady. If you took to it you'd be a fool; but I should have been a fool if I'd taken to anything else.

VIVIE. [*more and more deeply moved*] Mother: suppose we were both as poor as you were in those wretched old days, are you quite sure that you wouldn't advise me to try the Waterloo bar, or marry a laborer, or even go into the factory?

MRS. WARREN. [*indignantly*] Of course not. What sort of mother do you take me for! How could you keep your self-respect in such starvation and slavery? And what's a woman worth? what's life worth? without self-respect! Why am I independent and able to give my daughter a first-rate education, when other women that had just as good opportunities are in the gutter? Because I always knew how to respect myself and control myself. Why is Liz looked up to in a cathedral town? The same reason. Where would we be now if we'd minded the clergyman's foolishness? Scrubbing floors for one and sixpence a day and nothing to look forward to but the workhouse infirmary. Don't you be led astray by people who don't know the world, my girl. The only way for a woman to provide for herself decently is for her to be good to some man that can afford to be good to her. If she's in his own station of life, let her make him marry her; but if she's far beneath him she can't expect it: why should she? it wouldn't be for her own happiness. Ask any lady in London society that has daughters; and she'll tell you the same, except that I tell you straight and she'll tell you crooked. That's all the difference.

VIVIE. [*fascinated, gazing at her*] My dear mother: you are a wonderful woman: you are stronger than all England. And are you really and truly not one wee bit doubtful—or—or—ashamed?

MRS. WARREN. Well, of course, dearie, it's only good manners to be ashamed of it: it's expected from a woman. Women have to pretend to feel a great deal that they don't feel. Liz used to be angry with me for plumping out the truth about it. She used to say that when every woman could learn enough from what was going on in the world before her eyes, there was no need to talk about it to her. But then Liz was such a perfect lady! She had the true instinct of it; while I was always a bit of a vulgarian. I used to be so pleased when you sent me your photos to see that you were growing up like Liz: you've just her ladylike, determined way. But I can't stand saying one thing when everyone knows I mean another. What's the use in such hypocrisy? If people arrange the world that way for women, there's no good pretending it's arranged the other way. No: I never was a bit ashamed really. I consider I had a right to be proud of how we managed everything so respectably, and never had a word against us, and how the girls were so well taken care of. Some of them did very well: one of them married an ambassador. But of course now I daren't talk about such things: whatever would they think of us! [*She yawns*]. Oh dear! I do believe I'm getting sleepy after all. [*She stretches herself lazily, thoroughly relieved by her explosion, and placidly ready for her night's rest*].

VIVIE. I believe it is I who will not be able to sleep now. [She goes to the dresser and lights the candle. Then she extinguishes the lamp, darkening the room a good deal]. Better let in some fresh air before locking up. [*She opens the cottage door, and finds that it is broad moonlight*]. What a beautiful night! Look! [*She draws the curtains of the window. The landscape is seen bathed in the radiance of the harvest moon rising over Blackdown*].

MRS. WARREN. [*with a perfunctory glance at the scene*] Yes, dear; but take care you don't catch your death of cold from the night air.

VIVIE. [*contemptuously*] Nonsense.

MRS. WARREN. [querulously] Oh yes: everything I say is nonsense, according to you.

VIVIE. [*turning to her quickly*] No: really that is not so, mother. You have got completely the better of me tonight, though I intended it to be the other way. Let us be good friends now.

MRS. WARREN. [*shaking her head a little ruefully*] So it has been the other way. But I suppose I must give in to it. I always got the worst of it from Liz; and now I suppose it'll be the same with you.

VIVIE. Well, never mind. Come: good-night, dear old mother. [*She takes her mother in her arms*].

MRS. WARREN. [*fondly*] I brought you up well, didn't I, dearie?

VIVIE. You did.

MRS. WARREN. And you'll be good to your poor old mother for it, won't you?

VIVIE. I will, dear. [*Kissing her*] Good-night.

MRS. WARREN. [*with unction*] Blessings on my own dearie darling! a mother's blessing![She embraces her daughter protectingly, instinctively looking upward for divine sanction.]

ACT III

In the Rectory garden next morning, with the sun shining from a cloudless sky. The garden wall has a five-barred wooden gate, wide enough to admit a carriage, in the middle. Beside the gate hangs a bell on a coiled spring, communicating with a pull outside. The carriage drive comes down the middle of the garden and then swerves to its left, where it ends in a little gravelled circus opposite the Rectory porch. Beyond the gate is seen the dusty high road, parallel with the wall, bounded on the farther side by a strip of turf and an unfenced pine wood. On the lawn, between the house and the drive, is a clipped yew tree, with a garden bench in its shade. On the opposite side the garden is shut in by a box hedge; and there is a little sundial on the turf, with an iron chair near it. A little path leads through the box hedge, behind the sundial.

FRANK, seated on the chair near the sundial, on which he has placed the morning paper, is reading The Standard. His father comes from the house, red-eyed and shivery, and meets FRANK'S eye with misgiving.

FRANK. [*looking at his watch*] Half-past eleven. Nice your for a rector to come down to breakfast!

REV. S. Don't mock, Frank: don't mock. I am a little—er—[Shivering]—

FRANK. Off color?

REV. S. [*repudiating the expression*] No, sir: unwell this morning. Where's your mother?

FRANK. Don't be alarmed: she's not here. Gone to town by the 11.13 with Bessie. She left several messages for you. Do you feel equal to receiving them now, or shall I wait till you've breakfasted?

REV. S. I h a v e breakfasted, sir. I am surprised at your mother going to town when we have people staying with us. They'll think it very strange.

FRANK. Possibly she has considered that. At all events, if Crofts is going to stay here, and you are going to sit up every night with him until four, recalling the incidents of your fiery youth, it is clearly my mother's duty, as a prudent housekeeper, to go up to the stores and order a barrel of whisky and a few hundred siphons.

REV. S. I did not observe that Sir George drank excessively.

FRANK. You were not in a condition to, gov'nor.

REV. S. Do you mean to say that I—?

FRANK. [*calmly*] I never saw a beneficed clergyman less sober. The anecdotes you told about your past career were so awful that I really don't think Praed would have passed the night under your roof if it hadn't been for the way my mother and he took to one another.

REV. S. Nonsense, sir. I am Sir George Crofts' host. I must talk to him about something; and he has only one subject. Where is Mr. Praed now?

FRANK. He is driving my mother and Bessie to the station.

REV. S. Is Crofts up yet?

FRANK. Oh, long ago. He hasn't turned a hair: he's in much better practice than you. Has kept it up ever since, probably. He's taken himself off somewhere to smoke. [*FRANK resumes his paper. The parson turns disconsolately towards the gate; then comes back irresolutely.*]

REV. S. Er—Frank.

FRANK. Yes.

REV. S. Do you think the Warrens will expect to be asked here after yesterday afternoon?

FRANK. They've been asked already.

REV. S. [*appalled*] What!!!

FRANK. Crofts informed us at breakfast that you told him to bring Mrs. Warren and Vivie over here to-day, and to invite them to make this house their home. My mother then found she must go to town by the 11.13 train.

REV. S. [*with despairing vehemence*] I never gave any such invitation. I never thought of such a thing.

FRANK. [*compassionately*] How do you know, gov'nor, what you said and thought last night?

PRAED. [*coming in through the hedge*] Good morning.

REV. S. Good morning. I must apologize for not having met you at breakfast. I have a touch of—of—

FRANK. Clergyman's sore throat, Praed. Fortunately not chronic.

PRAED. [*changing the subject*] Well I must say your house is in a charming spot here. Really most charming.

REV. S. Yes: it is indeed. Frank will take you for a walk, Mr. Praed, if you like. I'll ask you to excuse me: I must take the opportunity to write my sermon while Mrs. Gardner is away and you are all amusing yourselves. You won't mind, will you?

PRAED. Certainly not. Don't stand on the slightest ceremony with me.

REV. S. Thank you. I'll—er—er—[*He stammers his way to the porch and vanishes into the house*].

PRAED. Curious thing it must be writing a sermon every week.

FRANK. Ever so curious, if he did it. He buys em. He's gone for some soda water.

PRAED. My dear boy: I wish you would be more respectful to your father. You know you can be so nice when you like.

FRANK. My dear Praddy: you forget that I have to live with the governor. When two people live together—it don't matter whether they're father and son or husband and wife or brother and sister—they can't keep up the polite humbug that's so easy for ten minutes on an afternoon call. Now the governor, who unites to many admirable domestic qualities the irresoluteness of a sheep and the pompousness and aggressiveness of a jackass—

PRAED. No, pray, pray, my dear Frank, remember! He is your father.

FRANK. I give him due credit for that. [*Rising and flinging down his paper*] But just imagine his telling Crofts to bring the Warrens over here! He must have been ever so drunk. You know, my dear Praddy, my mother wouldn't stand Mrs. Warren for a moment. Vivie mustn't come here until she's gone back to town.

PRAED. But your mother doesn't know anything about Mrs. Warren, does she? [*He picks up the paper and sits down to read it*].

FRANK. I don't know. Her journey to town looks as if she did. Not that my mother would mind in the ordinary way: she has stuck like a brick to lots of women who had got into trouble. But they were all nice women. That's what makes the real difference. Mrs. Warren, no doubt, has her merits; but she's ever so rowdy; and my mother simply wouldn't put up with her. So—hallo! [*This exclamation is provoked by the reappearance of the clergyman, who comes out of the house in haste and dismay*].

REV. S. Frank: Mrs. Warren and her daughter are coming across the heath with Crofts: I saw them from the study windows. What am I to say about your mother?

FRANK. Stick on your hat and go out and say how delighted you are to see them; and that Frank's in the garden; and that mother and Bessie have been called to the bedside of a sick relative, and were ever so sorry they couldn't stop; and that you hope Mrs. Warren slept well; and—and—say any blessed thing except the truth, and leave the rest to Providence.

REV. S. But how are we to get rid of them afterwards?

FRANK. There's no time to think of that now. Here! [*He bounds into the house*].

REV. S. He's so impetuous. I don't know what to do with him, Mr. Praed.

FRANK. [returning with a clerical felt hat, which he claps on his father's head]. Now: off with you. [Rushing him through the gate]. Praed and I'll wait here, to give the thing an unpremeditated air. [The clergyman, dazed but obedient, hurries off].

FRANK. We must get the old girl back to town somehow, Praed. Come! Honestly, dear Praddy, do you like seeing them together?

PRAED. Oh, why not?

FRANK. [his teeth on edge] Don't it make your flesh creep ever so little? that wicked old devil, up to every villainy under the sun, I'll swear, and Vivie—ugh!

PRAED. Hush, pray. They're coming. [The clergyman and CROFTS are seen coming along the road, followed by MRS. WARREN and VIVIE walking affectionately together.]

FRANK. Look: she actually has her arm round the old woman's waist. It's her right arm: she began it. She's gone sentimental, by God! Ugh! ugh! Now do you feel the creeps? [The clergyman opens the gate: and MRS. WARREN and VIVIE pass him and stand in the middle of the garden looking at the house. FRANK, in an ecstasy of dissimulation, turns gaily to MRS. WARREN, exclaiming] Ever so delighted to see you, Mrs. Warren. This quiet old rectory garden becomes you perfectly.

MRS. WARREN. Well, I never! Did you hear that, George? He says I look well in a quiet old rectory garden.

REV. S. [still holding the gate for CROFTS, who loafs through it, heavily bored] You look well everywhere, Mrs. Warren.

FRANK. Bravo, gov'nor! Now look here: lets have a treat before lunch. First lets see the church. Everyone has to do that. It's a regular old thirteenth century church, you know: the gov'nor's ever so fond of it, because he got up a restoration fund and had it completely rebuilt six years ago. Praed will be able to shew its points.

REV. S. [mooning hospitably at them] I shall be pleased, I'm sure, if Sir George and Mrs. Warren really care about it.

MRS. WARREN. Oh, come along and get it over.

CROFTS. [turning back toward the gate] I've no objection.

REV. S. Not that way. We go through the fields, if you don't mind. Round here. [He leads the way by the little path through the box hedge].

CROFTS. Oh, all right. [He goes with the parson. PRAED follows with MRS. WARREN. VIVIE does not stir: she watches them until they *have gone, with all the lines of purpose in her face marking it strongly.*]

FRANK. Ain't you coming?

VIVIE. No. I want to give you a warning, Frank. You were making fun of my mother just now when you said that about the rectory garden. That is barred in the future. Please treat my mother with as much respect as you treat your own.

FRANK. My dear Viv: she wouldn't appreciate it: the two cases require different treatment. But what on earth has happened to you? Last night we were perfectly agreed as to your mother and her set. This morning I find you attitudinizing sentimentally with your arm around your parent's waist.

VIVIE. [*flushing*] Attitudinizing!

FRANK. That was how it struck me. First time I ever saw you do a second-rate thing.

VIVIE. [*controlling herself*] Yes, Frank: there has been a change: but I don't think it a change for the worse. Yesterday I was a little prig.

FRANK. And today?

VIVIE. [*wincing; then looking at him steadily*] Today I know my mother better than you do.

FRANK. Heaven forbid!

VIVIE. What do you mean?

FRANK. Viv: there's a freemasonry among thoroughly immoral people that you know nothing of. You've too much character. That's the bond between your mother and me: that's why I know her better than you'll ever know her.

VIVIE. You are wrong: you know nothing about her. If you knew the circumstances against which my mother had to struggle—

FRANK. [*adroitly finishing the sentence for her*] I should know why she is what she is, shouldn't I? What difference would that make? Circumstances or no circumstances, Viv, you won't be able to stand your mother.

VIVIE. [*very angry*] Why not?

FRANK. Because she's an old wretch, Viv. If you ever put your arm around her waist in my presence again, I'll shoot myself there and then as a protest against an exhibition which revolts me.

VIVIE. Must I choose between dropping your acquaintance and dropping my mother's?

FRANK. [*gracefully*] That would put the old lady at ever such a disadvantage. No, Viv: your infatuated little boy will have to stick to you in any case. But he's all the more anxious that you shouldn't make mistakes. It's no use, Viv: your mother's impossible. She may be a good sort; but she's a bad lot, a very bad lot.

VIVIE. [*hotly*] Frank—! [*He stands his ground. She turns away and sits down on the bench under the yew tree, struggling to recover her self-command. Then she says*] Is she to be deserted by the world because she's what you call a bad lot? Has she no right to live?

FRANK. No fear of that, Viv: she won't ever be deserted. [*He sits on the bench beside her*].

VIVIE. But I am to desert her, I suppose.

FRANK. [*babyishly, lulling her and making love to her with his voice*] Mustn't go live with her. Little family group of mother and daughter wouldn't be a success. Spoil o u r little group.

VIVIE. [*falling under the spell*] What little group?

FRANK. The babes in the wood: Vivie and little Frank. [*He nestles against her like a weary child*]. Lets go and get covered up with leaves.

VIVIE. [*rhythmically, rocking him like a nurse*] Fast asleep, hand in hand, under the trees.

FRANK. The wise little girl with her silly little boy.

VIVIE. The deal little boy with his dowdy little girl.

FRANK. Ever so peaceful, and relieved from the imbecility of the little boy's father and the questionableness of the little girl's—

VIVIE. [*smothering the word against her breast*] Sh-sh-sh-sh! little girl wants to forget all about her mother. [*They are silent for some moments, rocking one another. Then VIVIE wakes up with a shock, exclaiming*] What a pair of fools we are! Come: sit up. Gracious! your hair. [*She smooths it*]. I wonder do all grown up people play in that childish way when nobody is looking. I never did it when I was a child.

FRANK. Neither did I. You are my first playmate. [*He catches her hand to kiss it, but checks himself to look around first. Very unexpectedly, he sees CROFTS emerging from the box hedge*]. Oh damn!

VIVIE. Why damn, dear?

FRANK. [*whispering*] Sh! Here's this brute Crofts. [*He sits farther away from her with an unconcerned air*].

CROFTS. Could I have a few words with you, Miss Vivie?

VIVIE. Certainly.

CROFTS. [*to FRANK*] You'll excuse me, Gardner. They're waiting for you in the church, if you don't mind.

FRANK. [*rising*] Anything to oblige you, Crofts—except church. If you should happen to want me, Vivvums, ring the gate bell. [*He goes into the house with unruffled suavity*].

CROFTS. [*watching him with a crafty air as he disappears, and speaking to VIVIE with an assumption of being on privileged terms with her*] Pleasant young fellow that, Miss Vivie. Pity he has no money, isn't it?

VIVIE. Do you think so?

CROFTS. Well, what's he to do? No profession. No property. What's he good for?

VIVIE. I realize his disadvantages, Sir George.

CROFTS. [*a little taken aback at being so precisely interpreted*] Oh, it's not that. But while we're in this world we're in it; and money's money. [*VIVIE does not answer*]. Nice day, isn't it?

VIVIE. [*with scarcely veiled contempt for this effort at conversation*] Very.

CROFTS. [*with brutal good humor, as if he liked her pluck*] Well that's not what I came to say. [*Sitting down beside her*] Now listen, Miss Vivie. I'm quite aware that I'm not a young lady's man.

VIVIE. Indeed, Sir George?

CROFTS. No; and to tell you the honest truth I don't want to be either. But when I say a thing I mean it; and when I feel a sentiment I feel it in earnest; and what I value I pay hard money for. That's the sort of man I am.

VIVIE. It does you great credit, I'm sure.

CROFTS. Oh, I don't mean to praise myself. I have my faults, Heaven knows: no man is more sensible of that than I am. I know I'm not perfect: that's one of the advantages of being a middle-aged man; for I'm not a young man, and I know it. But my code is a simple one, and, I think, a good one. Honor between man and man; fidelity between man and woman; and no can't about this religion or that religion, but an honest belief that things are making for good on the whole.

VIVIE. [*with biting irony*] "A power, not ourselves, that makes for righteousness," eh?

CROFTS. [*taking her seriously*] Oh certainly. Not ourselves, of course. Y o u understand what I mean. Well, now as to practical matters. You may have an idea that I've flung my money about; but I haven't: I'm richer today than when I first came into the property. I've used my knowledge of the world to invest my money in ways that other men have overlooked; and whatever else I may be, I'm a safe man from the money point of view.

VIVIE. It's very kind of you to tell me all this.

CROFTS. Oh well, come, Miss Vivie: you needn't pretend you don't see what I'm driving at. I want to settle down with a Lady Crofts. I suppose you think me very blunt, eh?

VIVIE. Not at all: I am very much obliged to you for being so definite and business-like. I quite appreciate the offer: the money, the position, Lady Crofts, and so on. But I think I will say no, if you don't mind, I'd rather not. [*She rises, and strolls across to the sundial to get out of his immediate neighborhood*].

CROFTS. [*not at all discouraged, and taking advantage of the additional room left him on the seat to spread himself comfortably, as if a few preliminary refusals were part of the inevitable routine of courtship*] I'm in no hurry. It was only just to let you know in case young Gardner should try to trap you. Leave the question open.

VIVIE. [*sharply*] My no is final. I won't go back from it. [*CROFTS is not impressed. He grins; leans forward with his elbows on his knees to prod with his stick at some unfortunate insect in the grass; and looks cunningly at her. She turns away impatiently.*]

CROFTS. I'm a good deal older than you. Twenty-five years: quarter of a century. I shan't live for ever; and I'll take care that you shall be well off when I'm gone.

VIVIE. I am proof against even that inducement, Sir George. Don't you think you'd better take your answer? There is not the slightest chance of my altering it.

CROFTS. [*rising, after a final slash at a daisy, and coming nearer to her*] Well, no matter. I could tell you some things that would change your mind fast enough; but I wont, because I'd rather win you by honest affection. I was a good friend to your mother: ask her whether I wasn't. She'd never have make the money that paid for your education if it hadn't been for my advice and help, not to mention the money I advanced her. There are not many men who would have stood by her as I have. I put not less than forty thousand pounds into it, from first to last.

VIVIE. [*staring at him*] Do you mean to say that you were my mother's business partner?

CROFTS. Yes. Now just think of all the trouble and the explanations it would save if we were to keep the whole thing in the family, so to speak. Ask your mother whether she'd like to have to explain all her affairs to a perfect stranger.

VIVIE. I see no difficulty, since I understand that the business is wound up, and the money invested.

CROFTS. [*stopping short, amazed*] Wound up! Wind up a business that's paying 35 per cent in the worst years! Not likely. Who told you that?

VIVIE. [*her color quite gone*] Do you mean that it is still—? [*She stops abruptly, and puts her hand on the sundial to support herself. Then she gets quickly to the iron chair and sits down*]. What business are you talking about?

CROFTS. Well, the fact is it's not what would considered exactly a high-class business in my set—the country set, you know—o u r set it will be if you think better of my offer. Not that there's any mystery about it: don't think that. Of course you know by your mother's being in it that it's perfectly straight and honest. I've known her for many years; and I can say of her that she'd cut off her hands sooner than touch anything that was not what it ought to be. I'll tell you all about it if you like. I don't know whether you've found in travelling how hard it is to find a really comfortable private hotel.

VIVIE. [*sickened, averting her face*] Yes: go on.

CROFTS. Well, that's all it is. Your mother has got a genius for managing such things. We've got two in Brussels, one in Ostend, one in Vienna, and two in Budapest. Of course there are others besides ourselves in it; but we hold most of the capital; and your mother's indispensable as managing director. You've noticed, I daresay, that she travels a good deal. But you see you can't mention such things in society. Once let out the word hotel and everybody thinks you keep a public-house. You wouldn't like people to say that of your mother, would you? That's why we're so reserved about it. By the way, you'll keep it to yourself, won't you? Since it's been a secret so long, it had better remain so.

VIVIE. And this is the business you invite me to join you in?

CROFTS. Oh no. My wife shan't be troubled with business. You'll not be in it more than you've always been.

VIVIE. I always been! What do you mean?

CROFTS. Only that you've always lived on it. It paid for your education and the dress you have on your back. Don't turn up your nose at business, Miss Vivie: where would your Newnhams and Girtons be without it?

VIVIE. [*rising, almost beside herself*] Take care. I know what this business is.

CROFTS. [*starting, with a suppressed oath*] Who told you?

VIVIE. Your partner. My mother.

CROFTS. [*black with rage*] The old—[*VIVIE looks quickly at him. He swallows the epithet and stands for a moment swearing and raging foully to himself. But he knows that his cue is to be sympathetic. He takes refuge in generous indignation.*] She ought to have had more consideration for you. I'd never have told you.

VIVIE. I think you would probably have told me when we were married: it would have been a convenient weapon to break me in with.

CROFTS. [*quite sincerely*] I never intended that. On my word as a gentleman I didn't.[*VIVIE wonders at him. Her sense of the irony of his protest cools and braces her. She replies with contemptuous self-possession.*]

VIVIE. It does not matter. I suppose you understand that when we leave here today our acquaintance ceases.

CROFTS. Why? Is it for helping your mother?

VIVIE. My mother was a very poor woman who had no reasonable choice but to do as she did. You were a rich gentleman; and you did the same for the sake of 35 per cent. You are a pretty common sort of scoundrel, I think. That is my opinion of you.

CROFTS. [*after a stare: not at all displeased, and much more at his ease on these FRANK terms than on their former ceremonious ones*] Ha! ha! ha! ha! Go it, little missie, go it: it doesn't hurt me and it amuses you. Why the devil shouldn't I invest my money that way? I take the interest on my capital like other people: I hope you don't think I dirty my own hands with the work. Come! you wouldn't refuse the acquaintance of my mother's cousin the Duke of Belgravia because some of the rents he gets are earned in queer ways. You wouldn't cut the Archbishop of Canterbury, I suppose, because the Ecclesiastical Commissioners have a few publicans and sinners among their tenants. Do you remember your Crofts scholarship at Newnham? Well, that was founded by my brother the M.P. He gets his 22 per cent out of a factory with 600 girls in it, and not one of them getting wages enough to live on. How d'ye suppose they manage when they have no family to fall back on? Ask your mother. And do you expect me to turn my back on 35 per cent when all the rest are pocketing what they can, like sensible men? No such fool! If you're going to pick and choose your acquaintances on moral principles, you'd better clear out of this country, unless you want to cut yourself out of all decent society.

VIVIE. [*conscience stricken*] You might go on to point out that I myself never asked where the money I spent came from. I believe I am just as bad as you.

CROFTS. [*greatly reassured*] Of course you are; and a very good thing too! What harm does it do after all? [*Rallying her jocularly*] So you don't think me such a scoundrel now you come to think it over. Eh?

VIVIE. I have shared profits with you: and I admitted you just now to the familiarity of knowing what I think of you.

CROFTS. [*with serious friendliness*] To be sure you did. You won't find me a bad sort: I don't go in for being superfine intellectually; but I've plenty of honest human feeling; and the old Crofts breed comes out in a sort of instinctive hatred of anything low, in which I'm sure you'll sympathize with me. Believe me, Miss Vivie, the world isn't such a bad place as the croakers make out. As long as you don't fly openly in the face of society, society doesn't ask any inconvenient questions; and it makes precious short work of the cads who do. There are no secrets better kept than the secrets everybody guesses. In the class of people I can introduce you to, no lady or gentleman would so far forget themselves as to discuss my business affairs or your mothers. No man can offer you a safer position.

VIVIE. [*studying him curiously*] I suppose you really think you're getting on famously with me.

CROFTS. Well, I hope I may flatter myself that you think better of me than you did at first.

VIVIE. [*quietly*] I hardly find you worth thinking about at all now. [*She rises and turns towards the gate, pausing on her way to contemplate him and say almost gently, but with intense conviction.*] When I think of the society that tolerates you, and the laws that protect you! when I think of how helpless nine out of ten young girls would be in the hands of you and my mother! the unmentionable woman and her capitalist bully—

CROFTS. [*livid*] Damn you!

VIVIE. You need not. I feel among the damned already.

[*She raises the latch of the gate to open it and go out. He follows her and puts his hand heavily on the top bar to prevent its opening.*]

CROFTS. [*panting with fury*] Do you think I'll put up with this from you, you young devil?

VIVIE. [*unmoved*] Be quiet. Some one will answer the bell. [*Without flinching a step she strikes the bell with the back of her hand. It clangs harshly; and he starts back involuntarily. Almost immediately FRANK appears at the porch with his rifle*].

FRANK. [*with cheerful politeness*] Will you have the rifle, Viv; or shall I operate?

VIVIE. Frank: have you been listening?

FRANK. [*coming down into the garden*] Only for the bell, I assure you; so that you shouldn't have to wait. I think I shewed great insight into your character, Crofts.

CROFTS. For two pins I'd take that gun from you and break it across your head.

FRANK. [*stalking him cautiously*] Pray don't. I'm ever so careless in handling firearms. Sure to be a fatal accident, with a reprimand from the coroner's jury for my negligence.

VIVIE. Put the rifle away, Frank: it's quite unnecessary.

FRANK. Quite right, Viv. Much more sportsmanlike to catch him in a trap. [*CROFTS, understanding the insult, makes a threatening movement*]. Crofts: there are fifteen cartridges in the magazine here; and I am a dead shot at the present distance and at an object of your size.

CROFTS. Oh, you needn't be afraid. I'm not going to touch you.

FRANK. Ever so magnanimous of you under the circumstances! Thank you.

CROFTS. I'll just tell you this before I go. It may interest you, since you're so fond of one another. Allow me, Mister Frank, to introduce you to your half-sister, the eldest daughter of the Reverend Samuel Gardner. Miss Vivie: you half-brother. Good morning! [*He goes out through the gate and along the road*].

FRANK. [*after a pause of stupefaction, raising the rifle*] You'll testify before the coroner that it's an accident, Viv. [*He takes aim at the retreating figure of CROFTS. VIVIE seizes the muzzle and pulls it round against her breast*].

VIVIE. Fire now. You may.

FRANK. [*dropping his end of the rifle hastily*] Stop! take care. [*She lets it go. It falls on the turf*]. Oh, you've given your little boy such a turn. Suppose it had gone off! ugh! [*He sinks on the garden seat, overcome*].

VIVIE. Suppose it had: do you think it would not have been a relief to have some sharp physical pain tearing through me?

FRANK. [*coaxingly*] Take it ever so easy, dear Viv. Remember: even if the rifle scared that fellow into telling the truth for the first time in his life, that only makes us the babes in the woods in earnest. [*He holds out his arms to her*]. Come and be covered up with leaves again.

VIVIE. [*with a cry of disgust*] Ah, not that, not that. You make all my flesh creep.

FRANK. Why, what's the matter?

VIVIE. Goodbye. [*She makes for the gate*].

FRANK. [*jumping up*] Hallo! Stop! Viv! Viv! [*She turns in the gateway*] Where are you going to? Where shall we find you?

VIVIE. At Honoria Fraser's chambers, 67 Chancery Lane, for the rest of my life. [*She goes off quickly in the opposite direction to that taken by CROFTS*].

FRANK. But I say—wait—dash it! [*He runs after her*].

ACT IV

Honoria Fraser's chambers in Chancery Lane. An office at the top of New Stone Buildings, with a plate-glass window, distempered walls, electric light, and a patent stove. Saturday afternoon. The chimneys of Lincoln's Inn and the western sky beyond are seen through the window. There is a double writing table in the middle of the room, with a cigar box, ash pans, and a portable electric reading lamp almost snowed up in heaps of papers and books. This table has knee holes and chairs right and left and is very untidy. The clerk's desk, closed and tidy, with its high stool, is against the wall, near a door communicating with the inner rooms. In the opposite wall is the door leading to the public corridor. Its upper panel is of opaque glass, lettered in black on the outside, FRASER AND WARREN. A baize screen hides the corner between this door and the window.]

FRANK, in a fashionable light-colored coaching suit, with his stick, gloves, and white hat in his hands, is pacing up and down in the office. Somebody tries the door with a key.

FRANK. [*calling*] Come in. It's not locked.

[*VIVIE comes in, in her hat and jacket. She stops and stares at him.*]

VIVIE. [*sternly*] What are you doing here?

FRANK. Waiting to see you. I've been here for hours. Is this the way you attend to your business? [*He puts his hat and stick on the table, and perches himself with a vault on the clerk's stool, looking at her with every appearance of being in a specially restless, teasing, flippant mood*].

VIVIE. I've been away exactly twenty minutes for a cup of tea. [*She takes off her hat and jacket and hangs them behind the screen*]. How did you get in?

FRANK. The staff had not left when I arrived. He's gone to play cricket on Primrose Hill. Why don't you employ a woman, and give your sex a chance?

VIVIE. What have you come for?

FRANK. [*springing off the stool and coming close to her*] Viv: lets go and enjoy the Saturday half-holiday somewhere, like the staff. What do you say to Richmond, and then a music hall, and a jolly supper?

VIVIE. Can't afford it. I shall put in another six hours work before I go to bed.

FRANK. Can't afford it, can't we? Aha! Look here. [*He takes out a handful of sovereigns and makes them chink*]. Gold, Viv: gold!

VIVIE. Where did you get it?

FRANK. Gambling, Viv: gambling. Poker.

VIVIE. Pah! It's meaner than stealing it. No: I'm not coming. [*She sits down to work at the table, with her back to the glass door, and begins turning over the papers*].

FRANK. [*remonstrating piteously*] But, my dear Viv, I want to talk to you ever so seriously.

VIVIE. Very well: sit down in Honoria's chair and talk here. I like ten minutes chat after tea. [*He murmurs*]. No use groaning: I'm inexorable. [*He takes the opposite seat disconsolately*]. Pass that cigar box, will you?

FRANK. [*pushing the cigar box across*] Nasty womanly habit. Nice men don't do it any longer.

VIVIE. Yes: they object to the smell in the office; and we've had to take to cigarets. See! [*She opens the box and takes out a cigaret, which she lights. She offers him one; but he shakes his head with a wry face. She settles herself comfortably in her chair, smoking*]. Go ahead.

FRANK. Well, I want to know what you've done—what arrangements you've made.

VIVIE. Everything was settled twenty minutes after I arrived here. Honoria has found the business too much for her this year; and she was on the point of sending for me and proposing a partnership when I walked in and told her I hadn't a farthing in the world. So I installed myself and packed her off for a fortnight's holiday. What happened at Haslemere when I left?

FRANK. Nothing at all. I said you'd gone to town on particular business.

VIVIE. Well?

FRANK. Well, either they were too flabbergasted to say anything, or else Crofts had prepared your mother. Anyhow, she didn't say anything; and Crofts didn't say anything; and Praddy only stared. After tea they got up and went; and I've not seen them since.

VIVIE. [*nodding placidly with one eye on a wreath of smoke*] That's all right.

FRANK. [*looking round disparagingly*] Do you intend to stick in this confounded place?

VIVIE. [*blowing the wreath decisively away, and sitting straight up*] Yes. These two days have given me back all my strength and self-possession. I will never take a holiday again as long as I live.

FRANK. [*with a very wry face*] Mps! You look quite happy. And as hard as nails.

VIVIE. [*grimly*] Well for me that I am!

FRANK. [*rising*] Look here, Viv: we must have an explanation. We parted the other day under a complete misunderstanding. [*He sits on the table, close to her*].

VIVIE. [*putting away the cigaret*] Well: clear it up.

FRANK. You remember what Crofts said.

VIVIE. Yes.

FRANK. That revelation was supposed to bring about a complete change in the nature of our feeling for one another. It placed us on the footing of brother and sister.

VIVIE. Yes.

FRANK. Have you ever had a brother?

VIVIE. No.

FRANK. Then you don't know what being brother and sister feels like? Now I have lots of sisters; and the fraternal feeling is quite familiar to me. I assure you my feeling for you is not the least in the world like it. The girls will go their way; I will go mine; and we shan't care if we never see one another again. That's brother and sister. But as to you, I can't be easy if I have to pass a week without seeing you. That's not brother and sister. Its exactly what I felt an hour before Crofts made his revelation. In short, dear Viv, it's love's young dream.

VIVIE. [*bitingly*] The same feeling, Frank, that brought your father to my mother's feet. Is that it?

FRANK. [*so revolted that he slips off the table for a moment*] I very strongly object, Viv, to have my feelings compared to any which the Reverend Samuel is capable of harboring; and I object still more to a comparison of you to your mother. [*Resuming his perch*] Besides, I don't believe the story. I have taxed my father with it, and obtained from him what I consider tantamount to a denial.

VIVIE. What did he say?

FRANK. He said he was sure there must be some mistake.

VIVIE. Do you believe him?

FRANK. I am prepared to take his word against Crofts'.

VIVIE. Does it make any difference? I mean in your imagination or conscience; for of course it makes no real difference.

FRANK. [*shaking his head*] None whatever to me.

VIVIE. Nor to me.

FRANK. [*staring*] But this is ever so surprising! [*He goes back to his chair*]. I thought our whole relations were altered in your imagination and conscience, as you put it, the moment those words were out of that brute's muzzle.

VIVIE. No: it was not that. I didn't believe him. I only wish I could.

FRANK. Eh?

VIVIE. I think brother and sister would be a very suitable relation for us.

FRANK. You really mean that?

VIVIE. Yes. It's the only relation I care for, even if we could afford any other. I mean that.

FRANK. [*raising his eyebrows like one on whom a new light has dawned, and rising with quite an effusion of chivalrous sentiment*] My dear Viv: why didn't you say so before? I am ever so sorry for persecuting you. I understand, of course.

VIVIE. [*puzzled*] Understand what?

FRANK. Oh, I'm not a fool in the ordinary sense: only in the Scriptural sense of doing all the things the wise man declared to be folly, after trying them himself on the most extensive scale. I see I am no longer Vivvums's little boy. Don't be alarmed: I shall never call you Vivvums again—at least unless you get tired of your new little boy, whoever he may be.

VIVIE. My new little boy!

FRANK. [*with conviction*] Must be a new little boy. Always happens that way. No other way, in fact.

VIVIE. None that you know of, fortunately for you. [*Someone knocks at the door.*]

FRANK. My curse upon yon caller, whoe'er he be!

VIVIE. It's Praed. He's going to Italy and wants to say goodbye. I asked him to call this afternoon. Go and let him in.

FRANK. We can continue our conversation after his departure for Italy. I'll stay him out. [*He goes to the door and opens it*]. How are you, Praddy? Delighted to see you. Come in. [*PRAED, dressed for travelling, comes in, in high spirits.*]

PRAED. How do you do, Miss Warren? [She presses his hand cordially, though a certain sentimentality in his high spirits jars upon her]. I start in an hour from Holborn Viaduct. I wish I could persuade you to try Italy.

VIVIE. What for?

PRAED. Why, to saturate yourself with beauty and romance, of course. [*VIVIE, with a shudder, turns her chair to the table, as if the work waiting for her there were a support to her. PRAED sits opposite to her. FRANK places a chair near VIVIE, and drops lazily and carelessly into it, talking at her over his shoulder.*]

FRANK. No use, Praddy. Viv is a little Philistine. She is indifferent to my romance, and insensible to my beauty.

VIVIE. Mr. Praed: once for all, there is no beauty and no romance in life for me. Life is what it is; and I am prepared to take it as it is.

PRAED. [*enthusiastically*] You will not say that if you come with me to Verona and on to Venice. You will cry with delight at living in such a beautiful world.

FRANK. This is most eloquent, Praddy. Keep it up.

PRAED. Oh, I assure you I have cried—I shall cry again, I hope—at fifty! At your age, Miss Warren, you would not need to go so far as Verona. Your spirits would absolutely fly up at the mere sight of Ostend. You would be charmed with the gaiety, the vivacity, the happy air of Brussels.

VIVIE. [*springing up with an exclamation of loathing*] Agh!

PRAED. [*rising*] What's the matter?

FRANK. [*rising*] Hallo, Viv!

VIVIE. [*to PRAED, with deep reproach*] Can you find no better example of your beauty and romance than Brussels to talk to me about?

PRAED. [*puzzled*] Of course it's very different from Verona. I don't suggest for a moment that—

VIVIE. [*bitterly*] Probably the beauty and romance come to much the same in both places.

PRAED. [*completely sobered and much concerned*] My dear Miss Warren: I—[*looking enquiringly at FRANK*] Is anything the matter?

FRANK. She thinks your enthusiasm frivolous, Praddy. She's had ever such a serious call.

VIVIE. [*sharply*] Hold your tongue, Frank. Don't be silly.

FRANK. [*sitting down*] Do you call this good manners, Praed?

PRAED. [*anxious and considerate*] Shall I take him away, Miss Warren? I feel sure we have disturbed you at your work.

VIVIE. Sit down: I'm not ready to go back to work yet. [*PRAED sits*]. You both think I have an attack of nerves. Not a bit of it. But there are two subjects I want dropped, if you don't mind. One of them [*to FRANK*] is love's young dream in any shape or form: the other [*to PRAED*] is the romance and beauty of life, especially Ostend and the gaiety of Brussels. You are welcome to any illusions you may have left on these subjects: I have none. If we three are to remain friends, I must be treated as a woman of business, permanently single [*to FRANK*] and permanently unromantic [*to PRAED*].

FRANK. I also shall remain permanently single until you change your mind. Praddy: change the subject. Be eloquent about something else.

PRAED. [*diffidently*] I'm afraid there's nothing else in the world that I can talk about. The Gospel of Art is the only one I can preach. I know Miss Warren is a great devotee of the Gospel of Getting On; but we can't discuss that without hurting your feelings, Frank, since you are determined not to get on.

FRANK. Oh, don't mind my feelings. Give me some improving advice by all means: it does me ever so much good. Have another try to make a successful man of me, Viv. Come: lets have it all: energy, thrift, foresight, self-respect, character. Don't you hate people who have no character, Viv?

VIVIE. [*wincing*] Oh, stop, stop. Let us have no more of that horrible cant. Mr. Praed: if there are really only those two gospels in the world, we had better all kill ourselves; for the same taint is in both, through and through.

FRANK. [*looking critically at her*] There is a touch of poetry about you today, Viv, which has hitherto been lacking.

PRAED. [*remonstrating*] My dear Frank: aren't you a little unsympathetic?

VIVIE. [*merciless to herself*] No: it's good for me. It keeps me from being sentimental.

FRANK. [*bantering her*] Checks your strong natural propensity that way, don't it?

VIVIE. [*almost hysterically*] Oh yes: go on: don't spare me. I was sentimental for one moment in my life—beautifully sentimental—by moonlight; and now—

FRANK. [*quickly*] I say, Viv: take care. Don't give yourself away.

VIVIE. Oh, do you think Mr. Praed does not know all about my mother? [Turning on PRAED] You had better have told me that morning, Mr. Praed. You are very old fashioned in your delicacies, after all.

PRAED. Surely it is you who are a little old fashioned in your prejudices, Miss Warren. I feel bound to tell you, speaking as an artist, and believing that the most intimate human relationships are far beyond and above the scope of the law, that though I know that your mother is an unmarried woman, I do not respect her the less on that account. I respect her more.

FRANK. [*airily*] Hear! hear!

VIVIE. [*staring at him*] Is that all you know?

PRAED. Certainly that is all.

VIVIE. Then you neither of you know anything. Your guesses are innocence itself compared with the truth.

PRAED. [*rising, startled and indignant, and preserving his politeness with an effort*] I hope not. [*More emphatically*] I hope not, Miss Warren.

FRANK. [*whistles*] Whew!

VIVIE. You are not making it easy for me to tell you, Mr. Praed.

PRAED. [*his chivalry drooping before their conviction*] If there is anything worse—that is, anything else—are you sure you are right to tell us, Miss Warren?

VIVIE. I am sure that if I had the courage I should spend the rest of my life in telling everybody—stamping and branding it into them until they all felt their part in its abomination as I feel mine. There is nothing I despise more than the wicked convention that protects these things by forbidding a woman to mention them. And yet I can't tell you. The two infamous words that describe what my mother is are ringing in my ears and struggling on my tongue; but I can't utter them: the shame of them is too horrible for me. [*She buries her face in her hands. The two men, astonished, stare at one another and then at her. She raises her head again desperately and snatches a sheet of paper and a pen*]. Here: let me draft you a prospectus.

FRANK. Oh, she's mad. Do you hear, Viv? mad. Come! pull yourself together.

VIVIE. You shall see. [*She writes*]. "Paid up capital: not less than forty thousand pounds standing in the name of Sir George Crofts, Baronet, the chief shareholder. Premises at Brussels, Ostend, Vienna, and Budapest. Managing director: Mrs. Warren"; and now don't let us forget h e r qualifications: the two words. [*She writes the words and pushes the paper to them*]. There! Oh no: don't read it: don't! [*She snatches it back and tears it to pieces; then seizes her head in her hands and hides her face on the table. FRANK, who has watched the writing over her shoulder, and opened his eyes very widely at it, takes a card from his pocket; scribbles the two words on it; and silently hands it to PRAED, who reads it with amazement, and hides it hastily in his pocket.*]

FRANK. [*whispering tenderly*] Viv, dear: that's all right. I read what you wrote: so did Praddy. We understand. And we remain, as this leaves us at present, yours ever so devotedly.

PRAED. We do indeed, Miss Warren. I declare you are the most splendidly courageous woman I ever met. [*This sentimental compliment braces VIVIE. She throws it away from her with an impatient shake, and forces herself to stand up, though not without some support from the table.*]

FRANK. Don't stir, Viv, if you don't want to. Take it easy.

VIVIE. Thank you. You an always depend on me for two things: not to cry and not to faint. [*She moves a few steps towards the door of the inner room, and stops close to PRAED to say*] I shall need much more courage than that when I tell my mother that we have come to a parting of the ways. Now I must go into the next room for a moment to make myself neat again, if you don't mind.

PRAED. Shall we go away?

VIVIE. No: I'll be back presently. Only for a moment. [*She goes into the other room, PRAED opening the door for her*].

PRAED. What an amazing revelation! I'm extremely disappointed in Crofts: I am indeed.

FRANK. I'm not in the least. I feel he's perfectly accounted for at last. But what a facer for me, Praddy! I can't marry her now.

PRAED. [*sternly*] Frank! [*The two look at one another, FRANK unruffled, PRAED deeply indignant*]. Let me tell you, Gardner, that if you desert her now you will behave very despicably.

FRANK. Good old Praddy! Ever chivalrous! But you mistake: it's not the moral aspect of the case: it's the money aspect. I really can't bring myself to touch the old woman's money now.

PRAED. And was that what you were going to marry on?

FRANK. What else? I haven't any money, nor the smallest turn for making it. If I married Viv now she would have to support me; and I should cost her more than I am worth.

PRAED. But surely a clever bright fellow like you can make something by your own brains.

FRANK. Oh yes, a little. [*He takes out his money again*]. I made all that yesterday in an hour and a half. But I made it in a highly speculative business. No, dear Praddy: even if Bessie and Georgina marry millionaires and the governor dies after cutting them off with a shilling, I shall have only four hundred a year. And he won't die until he's three score and ten: he hasn't originality enough. I shall be on short allowance for the next twenty years. No short allowance for Viv, if I can help it. I withdraw gracefully and leave the field to the gilded youth of England. So that settled. I shan't worry her about it: I'll just send her a little note after we're gone. She'll understand.

PRAED. [*grasping his hand*] Good fellow, Frank! I heartily beg your pardon. But must you never see her again?

FRANK. Never see her again! Hang it all, be reasonable. I shall come along as often as possible, and be her brother. I can not understand the absurd consequences you romantic people expect from the most ordinary transactions. [*A knock at the door*]. I wonder who this is. Would you mind opening the door? If it's a client it will look more respectable than if I appeared.

PRAED. Certainly. [*He goes to the door and opens it. FRANK sits down in VIVIE's chair to scribble a note*]. My dear Kitty: come in: come in. [*MRS. WARREN comes in, looking apprehensively around for VIVIE. She has done her best to make herself matronly and dignified. The brilliant hat is replaced by a sober bonnet, and the gay blouse covered by a costly black silk mantle. She is pitiably anxious and ill at ease: evidently panic-stricken.*]

MRS. WARREN. [to Frank] What! Y o u r e here, are you?

FRANK. [*turning in his chair from his writing, but not rising*] Here, and charmed to see you. You come like a breath of spring.

MRS. WARREN. Oh, get out with your nonsense. [*In a low voice*] Where's Vivie?

[*FRANK points expressively to the door of the inner room, but says nothing.*]

MRS. WARREN. [*sitting down suddenly and almost beginning to cry*] Praddy: won't she see me, don't you think?

PRAED. My dear Kitty: don't distress yourself. Why should she not?

MRS. WARREN. Oh, you never can see why not: you're too innocent. Mr. Frank: did she say anything to you?

FRANK. [*folding his note*] She must see you, if [*very expressively*] you wait till she comes in.

MRS. WARREN. [*frightened*] Why shouldn't I wait?

[*FRANK looks quizzically at her; puts his note carefully on the ink-bottle, so that VIVIE cannot fail to find it when next she dips her pen; then rises and devotes his attention entirely to her.*]

FRANK. My dear Mrs. Warren: suppose you were a sparrow—ever so tiny and pretty a sparrow hopping in the roadway—and you saw a steam roller coming in your direction, would you wait for it?

MRS. WARREN. Oh, don't bother me with your sparrows. What did she run away from Haslemere like that for?

FRANK. I'm afraid she'll tell you if you rashly await her return.

MRS. WARREN. Do you want me to go away?

FRANK. No: I always want you to stay. But I advise you to go away.

MRS. WARREN. What! And never see her again!

FRANK. Precisely.

MRS. WARREN. [*crying again*] Praddy: don't let him be cruel to me. [*She hastily checks her tears and wipes her eyes*]. She'll be so angry if she sees I've been crying.

FRANK. [*with a touch of real compassion in his airy tenderness*] You know that Praddy is the soul of kindness, Mrs. Warren. Praddy: what do you say? Go or stay?

PRAED. [*to MRS. WARREN*] I really should be very sorry to cause you unnecessary pain; but I think perhaps you had better not wait. The fact is—[*VIVIE is heard at the inner door*].

FRANK. Sh! Too late. She's coming.

MRS. WARREN. Don't tell her I was crying. [*VIVIE comes in. She stops gravely on seeing MRS. WARREN, who greets her with hysterical cheerfulness*]. Well, dearie. So here you are at last.

VIVIE. I am glad you have come: I want to speak to you. You said you were going, Frank, I think.

FRANK. Yes. Will you come with me, Mrs. Warren? What do you say to a trip to Richmond, and the theatre in the evening? There is safety in Richmond. No steam roller there.

VIVIE. Nonsense, Frank. My mother will stay here.

MRS. WARREN. [*scared*] I don't know: perhaps I'd better go. We're disturbing you at your work.

VIVIE. [*with quiet decision*] Mr. Praed: please take Frank away. Sit down, mother. [*MRS. WARREN obeys helplessly*].

PRAED. Come, Frank. Goodbye, Miss Vivie.

VIVIE. [*shaking hands*] Goodbye. A pleasant trip.

PRAED. Thank you: thank you. I hope so.

FRANK. [*to MRS. WARREN*] Goodbye: you'd ever so much better have taken my advice. [*He shakes hands with her. Then airily to VIVIE*] Bye bye, Viv.

VIVIE. Goodbye. [*He goes out gaily without shaking hands with her*].

MRS. WARREN. Well, Vivie, what did you go away like that for without saying a word to me! How could you do such a thing! And what have you done to poor George? I wanted him to come with me; but he shuffled out of it. I could see that he was quite afraid of you. Only fancy: he wanted me not to come. As if [*trembling*] I should be afraid of you, dearie. [*VIVIE's gravity deepens*]. But of course I told him it was all settled and comfortable between us, and that we were on the best of terms. [*She breaks down*]. Vivie: what's the meaning of this? [*She produces a commercial envelope, and fumbles at the enclosure with trembling fingers*]. I got it from the bank this morning.

VIVIE. It is my month's allowance. They sent it to me as usual the other day. I simply sent it back to be placed to your credit, and asked them to send you the lodgment receipt. In future I shall support myself.

MRS. WARREN. [*not daring to understand*] Wasn't it enough? Why didn't you tell me? [*With a cunning gleam in her eye*] I'll double it: I was intending to double it. Only let me know how much you want.

VIVIE. You know very well that that has nothing to do with it. From this time I go my own way in my own business and among my own friends. And you will go yours. [*She rises*]. Goodbye.

MRS. WARREN. [*rising, appalled*] Goodbye?

VIVIE. Yes: goodbye. Come: don't let us make a useless scene: you understand perfectly well. Sir George Crofts has told me the whole business.

MRS. WARREN. [*angrily*] Silly old—[*She swallows an epithet, and then turns white at the narrowness of her escape from uttering it*].

VIVIE. Just so.

MRS. WARREN. He ought to have his tongue cut out. But I thought it was ended: you said you didn't mind.

VIVIE. [*steadfastly*] Excuse me: I do mind. You explained how it came about. That does not alter it.

[*MRS. WARREN, silenced for a moment, looks forlornly at VIVIE, who waits, secretly hoping that the combat is over. But the cunning expression comes back into MRS. WARREN's face; and she bends across the table, sly and urgent, half whispering.*]

MRS. WARREN. Vivie: do you know how rich I am?

VIVIE. I have no doubt you are very rich.

MRS. WARREN. But you don't know all that that means; you're too young. It means a new dress every day; it means theatres and balls every night; it means having the pick of all the gentlemen in Europe at your feet; it means a lovely house and plenty of servants; it means the choicest of eating and drinking; it means everything you like, everything you want, everything you can think of. And what are you here? A mere drudge, toiling and moiling early and late for your bare living and two cheap dresses a year. Think over it. [*Soothingly*] You're shocked, I know. I can enter into your feelings; and I think they do you credit; but trust me, nobody will blame you: you may take my word for that. I know what young girls are; and I know you'll think better of it when you've turned it over in your mind.

VIVIE. So that's how it is done, is it? You must have said all that to many a woman, to have it so pat.

MRS. WARREN. [*passionately*] What harm am I asking you to do? [*VIVIE turns away contemptuously. MRS. WARREN continues desperately*] Vivie: listen to me: you don't understand: you were taught wrong on purpose: you don't know what the world is really like.

VIVIE. [*arrested*] Taught wrong on purpose! What do you mean?

MRS. WARREN. I mean that you're throwing away all your chances for nothing. You think that people are what they pretend to be: that the way you were taught at school and college to think right and proper is the way things really are. But it's not: it's all only a pretence, to keep the cowardly slavish common run of people quiet. Do you want to find that out, like other women, at forty, when you've thrown yourself away and lost your chances; or won't you take it in good time now from your own mother, that loves you and swears to you that it's truth: gospel truth? [*Urgently*] Vivie: the big people, the clever people, the managing people, all know it. They do as I do, and think what I think. I know plenty of them. I know them to speak to, to introduce you to, to make friends of for you. I don't mean anything wrong: that's what you don't understand: your head is full of ignorant ideas about me. What do the people that taught you know about life or about people like me? When did they ever meet me, or speak to me, or let anyone tell them about me? the fools! Would they ever have done anything for you if I hadn't paid them? Haven't I told you that I want you to be respectable? Haven't I brought you up to be respectable? And how can you keep it up without my money and my influence and Lizzie's friends? Can't you see that you're cutting your own throat as well as breaking my heart in turning your back on me?

VIVIE. I recognize the Crofts philosophy of life, mother. I heard it all from him that day at the Gardners'.

MRS. WARREN. You think I want to force that played-out old sot on you! I don't, Vivie: on my oath I don't.

VIVIE. It would not matter if you did: you would not succeed. [*MRS. WARREN winces, deeply hurt by the implied indifference towards her affectionate intention. VIVIE, neither understanding this nor concerning herself about it, goes on calmly*] Mother: you don't at all know the sort of person I am. I don't object to Crofts more than to any other coarsely built man of his class. To tell you the truth, I rather admire him for being strong-minded enough to enjoy himself in his own way and make plenty of money instead of living the usual shooting, hunting, dining-out, tailoring, loafing life of his set merely because all the rest do it. And I'm perfectly aware that if I'd been in the same circumstances as my aunt Liz, I'd have done exactly what she did. I don't think I'm more prejudiced or straitlaced than you: I think I'm less. I'm certain I'm less sentimental. I know very well that fashionable morality is all a pretence, and that if I took your money and devoted the rest of my life to spending it fashionably, I might be as worthless and vicious as the silliest woman could possibly be without having a word said to me about it. But I don't want to be worthless. I shouldn't enjoy trotting about the park to advertise my dressmaker and carriage builder, or being bored at the opera to shew off a shop windowful of diamonds.

MRS. WARREN. [*bewildered*] But—

VIVIE. Wait a moment: I've not done. Tell me why you continue your business now that you are independent of it. Your sister, you told me, has left all that behind her. Why don't you do the same?

MRS. WARREN. Oh, it's all very easy for Liz: she likes good society, and has the air of being a lady. Imagine me in a cathedral town! Why, the very rooks in the trees would find me out even if I could stand the dulness of it. I must have work and excitement, or I should go melancholy mad. And what else is there for me to do? The life suits me: I'm fit for it and not for anything else. If I didn't do it somebody else would; so I don't do any real harm by it. And then it brings in money; and I like making money. No: it's no use: I can't give it up—not for anybody. But what need you know about it? I'll never mention it. I'll keep Crofts away. I'll not trouble you much: you see I have to be constantly running about from one place to another. You'll be quit of me altogether when I die.

VIVIE. No: I am my mother's daughter. I am like you: I must have work, and must make more money than I spend. But my work is not your work, and my way is not your way. We must part. It will not make much difference to us: instead of meeting one another for perhaps a few months in twenty years, we shall never meet: that's all.

MRS. WARREN. [*her voice stifled in tears*] Vivie: I meant to have been more with you: I did indeed.

VIVIE. It's no use, mother: I am not to be changed by a few cheap tears and entreaties any more than you are, I daresay.

MRS. WARREN. [*wildly*] Oh, you call a mother's tears cheap.

VIVIE. They cost you nothing; and you ask me to give you the peace and quietness of my whole life in exchange for them. What use would my company be to you if you could get it? What have we two in common that could make either of us happy together?

MRS. WARREN. [*lapsing recklessly into her dialect*] We're mother and daughter. I want my daughter. I've a right to you. Who is to care for me when I'm old? Plenty of girls have taken to me like daughters and cried at leaving me; but I let them all go because I had you to look forward to. I kept myself lonely for you. You've no right to turn on me now and refuse to do your duty as a daughter.

VIVIE. [*jarred and antagonized by the echo of the slums in her mother's voice*] My duty as a daughter! I thought we should come to that presently. Now once for all, mother, you want a daughter and Frank wants a wife. I don't want a mother; and I don't want a husband. I have spared neither Frank nor myself in sending him about his business. Do you think I will spare you?

MRS. WARREN. [*violently*] Oh, I know the sort you are: no mercy for yourself or anyone else. I know. My experience has done that for me anyhow: I can tell the pious, canting, hard, selfish woman when I meet her. Well, keep yourself to yourself: I don't want you. But listen to this. Do you know what I would do with you if you were a baby again? aye, as sure as there's a Heaven above us.

VIVIE. Strangle me, perhaps.

MRS. WARREN. No: I'd bring you up to be a real daughter to me, and not what you are now, with your pride and your prejudices and the college education you stole from me: yes, stole: deny it if you can: what was it but stealing? I'd bring you up in my own house, I would.

VIVIE. [*quietly*] In one of your own houses.

MRS. WARREN. [*screaming*] Listen to her! listen to how she spits on her mother's grey hairs! Oh, may you live to have your own daughter tear and trample on you as you have trampled on me. And you will: you will. No woman ever had luck with a mother's curse on her.

VIVIE. I wish you wouldn't rant, mother. It only hardens me. Come: I suppose I am the only young woman you ever had in your power that you did good to. Don't spoil it all now.

MRS. WARREN. Yes, Heaven forgive me, it's true; and you are the only one that ever turned on me. Oh, the injustice of it! the injustice! the injustice! I always wanted to be a good woman. I tried honest work; and I was slave-driven until I cursed the day I ever heard of honest work. I was a good mother; and because I made my daughter a good woman she turns me out as if I were a leper. Oh, if I only had my life to live over again! I'd talk to that lying clergyman in the school. From this time forth, so help me Heaven in my last hour, I'll do wrong and nothing but wrong. And I'll prosper on it.

VIVIE. Yes: it's better to choose your line and go through with it. If I had been you, mother, I might have done as you did; but I should not have lived one life and believed in another. You are a conventional woman at heart. That is why I am bidding you goodbye now. I am right, am I not?

MRS. WARREN. [*taken aback*] Right to throw away all my money!

VIVIE. No: right to get rid of you? I should be a fool not to. Isn't that so?

MRS. WARREN. [*sulkily*] Oh well, yes, if you come to that, I suppose you are. But Lord help the world if everybody took to doing the right thing! And now I'd better go than stay where I'm not wanted. [*She turns to the door*].

VIVIE. [*kindly*] Won't you shake hands?

MRS. WARREN. [after *looking at her fiercely for a moment with a savage impulse to strike her*] No, thank you. Goodbye.

VIVIE. [*matter-of-factly*] Goodbye. [*MRS. WARREN goes out, slamming the door behind her. The strain on VIVIE's face relaxes; her grave expression breaks up into one of joyous content; her breath goes out in a half sob, half laugh of intense relief. She goes buoyantly to her place at the writing table; pushes the electric lamp out of the way; pulls over a great sheaf of papers; and is in the act of dipping her pen in the ink when she finds FRANK's note. She opens it unconcernedly and reads it quickly, giving a little laugh at some quaint turn of expression in it*]. And goodbye, Frank. [*She tears the note up and tosses the pieces into the wastepaper basket without a second thought. Then she goes at her work with a plunge, and soon becomes absorbed in its figures*].

THE END

Printed in the United States
129018LV00007B/11/A